Time's Reservoir
A Quabbin Quills Anthology

Perpetual Imagination
Boston • Northampton • New York

881 Main St #10
Fitchburg, MA 01420

info@perpetualimagination.com

Manufactured in The United States of America.

1 2 3 4 5 6 7 8 9 10

First Edition

ISBN-10: 0692995153
ISBN-13: 978-0692995150

Library of Congress Control Number in process for this title.

Collecting

deep in the valley
walled up on all sides
sits the pool
collecting rain
deposited there
sectioned off
from the rest
isolating

this hidden oasis
in the forest
measuring rainfall
like hourglass sand

precious moments
locked in still waters
reflecting perfectly
my time here
mimicking the pool

a liquid photograph
of watery film
a brief documentary

say it to the trees
leave no stone
let the pool collect
memories too

a soft whisper
I was here

--Quabbin Quills, 2017

CONTENTS

THE MAN WHO USED TREES
Miryam Ehrlich Williamson

Charley Harvey was sitting under an old oak tree, just sitting, doing nothing. He was, if anything, waiting for the next thing to happen. He had a major stake in what that thing would be, and not even the slightest idea of what he might do to affect the outcome, one way or the other.

The tree wasn't working for Charley the way trees used to work, before this. Charley used trees the way people use tobacco or pot to draw away accumulated poisons, to soothe. Charley, it seemed, had used his last tree. Now whatever lay ahead didn't matter, the most of it was over.

Charley found out about trees and himself when he was ten, a dull-seeming boy with little capacity for fun or communication. His parents, both teachers, worked hard all day, drank even harder at night, and fell asleep in their easy chairs with their clothes on most nights. Charley didn't think he had been abused. If you're going to abuse a boy, first you have to notice him.

It happened one late afternoon when Charley came home from raking a neighbor's leaves, hungry. He didn't expect to find a meal set out for him. His parents, if they were home yet, would be "unwinding," as they put it, before thinking about dinner. Sometimes that's all they did about dinner -- think about it. Sometimes they actually ate together, but that was usually more by chance than by intention.

Charley thought he'd make a couple of salami sandwiches. The milk would probably be sour. His parents didn't put milk in their coffee, so they didn't know when it turned bad. When it went, Charley would pour it down the sink, and one parent or the other would eventually notice it was gone and buy another bottle. If there was no milk, Charley would open a can of tomato juice. One thing he could count on finding in the house was tomato juice. His parents drank it a lot, with vodka in it.

This time in the refrigerator famished Charley found nothing to eat. No salami, but there was mustard. No baloney, no corned beef, no American cheese, no goddamn tuna fish. Mustard and mayonnaise and ketchup and freaking Worcestershire sauce and not a goddamn fucking thing to put them on. With a surge of energy Charley slammed the refrigerator door so it rattled the cans and bottles stacked on top. He blew out of the kitchen door almost before he opened it, stalked across the backyard lawn, and flopped under the oak tree at the corner of the yard, breathing hard.

Charley was frightened by the way he was feeling. He feared he might explode from all the feeling he was doing. He couldn't hold still; lying on his back was impossible, as though the whole front of his body needed to be held in against the blast. He sat up, knees bent to his chest, and leaned back against the cool tree trunk, his breathing slowing.

Ten years later he would try to explain to Arielle what that tree did to him. "It poured itself into me," he would say. "It fed me. I wasn't hungry anymore, I wasn't aching, after a while I didn't hate my parents for being drunks. That tree took all the hurting anger out of me and put something calmer in its place." Arielle said she understood, but she didn't, she never got it.

Charley and Arielle got married and started making babies. Making them was easy and fun, paying for them was neither. Their house, at the end of a dirt road in the country, was rented from an old woman in the village who cared more that they took good care of the place than that they paid the going rate for rent in the area. Charlie had two jobs, and Arielle started taking in other people's kids for daycare. It was a good place to have kids. A grassy fenced-in yard surrounded by trees.

Charley didn't like the house much. It took a lot of fixing to keep it the way the owner wanted it, and she came by unannounced whenever it came into her mind to do so. But they'd have to pay half again as much rent if they moved, and Charley thought the trees were just fine. They did for him what the oak at his parents' place had done. When he and Arielle got to fighting, he'd walk out the kitchen door before things got out of hand and go sit up against one of the trees. So far the fighting was only just words, her words more than his. When he felt his muscles tighten and his breath speed up and his fingers curl in toward his palms, he'd go out the back door and pick a tree.

The school bus didn't come out as far as where Charley and Arielle and their kids lived, so when the oldest was ready to start school they moved into the village. Charley knew they were going to be house poor for years, but Arielle's logic was irrefutable: it was a rent-to-own deal and part of the rent, including all of the increase, went toward their down payment on the house. If they didn't move into town they'd need another car, and cars lose their value the minute you drive off the lot. A house adds some value each year. There was only one tree, and it stood by the side of the road on land the state-owned, but if he sat with his back to the road Charley could get its comfort. It didn't matter if the tree wasn't his or his landlord's.

The first thing the state did when they started to widen the road was cut down the tree. Charley, dressing for work, saw the men jump off the truck and put on hard hats. One of them grabbed a chainsaw while the other set out orange cones and "Men Working" signs. Barely half dressed, Charley tried to stop the men. They had their job to do, though. The sound of the saw ripped through Charley's chest, then his head.

Charley put the car in position, its nose pointing straight at the tree workers. He started the engine and, kneeling outside, released the emergency brake, wedged the gas pedal down with a piece of two-by-four, and rolled out of the way.

Now Charley Harvey is sitting under an old oak tree down the street from his house, just sitting, doing nothing. He is, if anything, waiting for the next thing to happen. He has a major stake in what that thing will be, and not even the slightest idea of what he might do to affect the outcome, one way or the other.

HANDS ACROSS TIME
Sally Sennott

My father was missing a finger, cut off down to the knuckle, or so I remembered. When I checked with my kid sister for details though, she clarified the memory. Dad had a disfigured index finger on his right hand that he couldn't straighten. Folklore has it that he fainted in the train on his way to Wentworth Institute of Technology where he was a student. When he went down he hit the radiator and scalded his finger, the steam also burning a half inch wide scar that ran down the back of his hand from index finger to wrist bone.

Dad used his hands to pump gas at the station he owned, to mow the grass, to fix small machinery, to wallpaper and paint, plumb and do electrical work. After a mid-life career change, he became a successful real estate broker. Now, he used his hands to keep track of his gas mileage and to run the calculator he carried in his suit pocket.

In this new role, Dad cooperated with my mother. Her hands were capable and sturdy. Using a metal file, she shaped her nails into neat points. Mom's fingernails were never painted or her hands bejeweled except for her wedding ring. It was she who ran the typewriter that filled in the blanks of the agreement when he sold a house or commercial property. She would pull the handle on the old fashioned adding machine and strike the keys on the IBM Selectric. Mom kept the books and typed out the tax forms and letters. They were a team, dedicated to both raising us girls and running the business.

At home, she used her hands to cook and can vegetables, run the vacuum and washing machine, and once a week to drive the car to do errands. In between these tasks, she bandaged bruises, fed the pets, and hung out the wet clothes in all weather. She ironed the laundry and ran the sheets through the mangle along with dad's boxer shorts and cloth handkerchiefs.

Dad ruled the household with an iron hand. Wife and children alike were under his dictatorial thumb. On occasion, he would use his hand to spank us kids, and on winter nights he would turn up the heat to 75 degrees after a cold day at the gas station. We children wilted in the forced hot air heat. Hands were seldom used for hugging or touching. One time he locked my mother out of the house for having the audacity to get a job outside of the home. It was an old-fashioned marriage, reflecting a time when gender equality was only a dream.

My husband was missing the fourth finger on his right hand. It was cut down to the knuckle by a malfunctioning wood splitting machine. He was logging when it happened, and he drove the cordwood truck to the hospital to get stitched up.

As a Marine, he qualified as an expert marksman. He used his strong and capable hands to shoot and wrestle, and to play poker with the guys. After our marriage, I taught him to play bridge, and he became a skilled duplicate player. He was in his element when wallpapering, painting and sanding floors. Over the years he built two saunas and fixed up houses for resale. When managing hotels, he dictated letters and used his hands to direct people.

At home, he spanked the kids and tilled the land to grow vegetables and flowers. He had a pot garden. He liked to stroke nylon when making love to me. At first, he ruled the roost with an iron hand like the generations of men before him. He signed the checks and made the big decisions.

As a bride, my hands were small and comely, and I wore long white gloves on my wedding day. My nails grew strong and long and rarely broke. In old age, the whites of my fingernails turned yellow and brittle and sometimes cracked. Still, my hands were sturdy and capable like my mother's. I used them to cook and sew, garden and make love, to hug the children and write on the chalkboard; to type, take notes and drive my own car, and make my way in the world of work.

As an educated, employed woman I made strides in a man's world. I lived out my feminist views. We were divorced and remarried several times before finding accord. By the age of 50, my husband was putting groceries in the cart and cooking all the meals. He fondly liked to call me "Miss Lemon" his personal assistant (after Hercule Poirot's personal secretary). He turned the checkbook over to me and I had an active role in decision making.

Our hands intertwined and we were able to find strength and resilience in our union. Like mom and dad before us we were a team, but the power dynamic was more in balance. As the years passed our relationship evolved into a marriage of equals. Our partnership reflected the triumphs and struggles we experienced.

Hands across time sculpt complex relationships and hold the makings of generational change. They craft the choices we make and their motions touch on society's transformation as well. While we are busy working and playing, our hands collect the stories of our lives.

VESSELS, PESTLES, LAKES AND MORTAR
Steve Michaels

The mortar was empty
It hadn't been used.
This vessel for the pestle,
In which potions brew,
Lay in two hands
Withered with age,
Belonging to one many considered a sage.

"Down in the lake, now a reservoir,
Stands a Lady of Fortune, Virtue, and War,"
Said the apothecary, a weary old fellow,
To the man who was searching for his timely castle.
"She'll give you a gatekey in the shape of a sword.
What you do with the weapon is your own accord."

And the man, much obliged, continued his journey
In search of the lady, the lake, and the gatekey.

He travelled the realm
And he thought of the mortar:
The empty container
In the Apoth's chamber.

The potential for potions and tricks of all kinds,
Pulsated throughout the vessel's tin sides.

And the questor did pause in the midst of the quest
To pondered a return to the medicine man's chest.

Why seek a kingdom whose walls will grow bare?
He thought as he stood between here and there.
What if my palace should prove just as hollow
As the mortar belonging to that fine fellow?
Perhaps if I take the symbol much further,
I'll transform my castle into a girder;
For we can have knowledge built upon strength.
And we can weave tales for the lessons we've spent.
We can gather round tables
Create legends galore.
Yes, I believe my kingdom can be more

These were his thoughts as he went to the lake.
And stood at the shore to study its wake.

And the lake where he stood
Is a watershed now
Where stories and legends and myths abound.

So whatever your opinion of Camelot's lot.
Tales hold up
For better or not.

For Arthur had seen the potential which grew,
From the mortar and pestle that all men can brew.

DAD WAS AHEAD OF HIS TIME
Phyllis Cochran

In 1949, when I was eleven years old, our family struggled through some tough times financially. Dad was a proud man and never asked for help from anyone. Instead, he headed for his workshop in our old barn in our hometown of Winchendon, Massachusetts.

There, he labored. We kept our distance and had no idea what he was doing for long periods of time. That was until he walked through the kitchen door one afternoon with a craft in hand. He held up the yellow object in the form of a hanging teapot. The handmade wooden design had been covered with yellow Formica and in the center was a decal. Near the base, hooks were screwed into place to hold three potholders. The teapot would hang on the wall.

"Dad is making these to sell," Mom explained. "They will come in four colors, red, yellow, blue and green. We'll need you three older girls to help. You'll be responsible for weaving the potholders." She handed each of us a metal frame and bags of cotton loops for weaving.

All summer we wove potholders to match the teapots. In the background, popular tunes blared from the radio. When our friends came to play, they joined us in weaving potholders. No one complained but seemed excited about Dad's craftsmanship. We each had our part to do and never goofed off.

"I'll go door to door in the neighborhood and take orders when enough potholders are finished," Mom stated. "Phyllis, you'll stay home and watch your little sister." Joyce was two years old at this time. I had helped care for her since her birth.

My sister Carol, two years younger than me, would help Mom with the sales. My older brother and two cousins that Mom and Dad were raising would help out on the home front when needed while Dad worked in the barn.

Since we had no car, Mom and my sister trudged along country roads, up hills and on hot summer days would stop for a cold drink at a nearby food store. Returning home, Mom smiled. "We sold lots of teapots. Red is the favorite color. We have orders for colors we ran out of."

After Mom felt she had depleted sales in our small town, she and my sister boarded a bus for the next town -- Gardner, Massachusetts, ten miles away. They hiked up many streets and along dirt roads hoping to make more sales.

"People are ordering more than one teapot. Some are planning to give them as gifts," Mom told us one especially productive day. "We've received many compliments on Dad's creativity. Next, we'll take the bus to Fitchburg."

There was no stopping Mom. I couldn't imagine how difficult it must be lugging the merchandise to deliver the orders or how Mom remembered the addresses of customers. "Oh," she said when asked, "Your sister is my helper. She has a wonderful memory and sense of direction."

Before long, Dad walked in from the barn to show us a napkin holder he'd designed. On both ends, a hole was drilled to fit small plastic salt and pepper shakers. The napkin holders would match the teapots making a set. Mom and Carol continued making sales until Dad went back to work.

Today my younger sister owns the old family homestead where the barn sits empty. Dad's workbench is gone, but Carol salvaged some teapot and napkin holder sets.

Now when I aimlessly walk through aisles of handmade crafts in auditoriums or outside in fields, I admire each item considering how much time went into producing it. I can't help but think Dad was ahead of his time.

This memory doesn't seem so long ago now. For me, these were the Good Old Days when our family worked together as a team.

SIMPLE GIFT
Diane Kane

Simple gift of words I give
to a man of simple birth.
In my life you've given me
treasures of priceless worth.

It's you who cast the mold
set solid to be my mind.
You who carved the lines
run through my soul I find.

Working the shapeless clay
with love to make my heart.
Artist skill you held the brush
on the canvas to set me apart.

It is you, the patient gardener
tending while I have grown.
The fruits of my life, many
the seeds you have sown.

Steady but gentle hand
when need for me to hold.
Words few and wisdom much
you taught me to stand bold.

Seeking long the rainbows end
your ageless spirit inspired me.
Making real the magic of life
believing in things I cannot see.

Sharing a sky of infinite stars
looking beyond walls of my mind.
Endless passion for living
love of adventures to find.

It's you I have to thank
treasures of a lifetime had.
You the man of many talents
the man I'm lucky to call Dad.

GETTING IT RIGHT
Sharon A. Harmon

Can you keep your muffins from sticking?

'Sounds like a personal problem to me,' I thought, shifting my butt on the sticky vinyl fifties-style chair. It was just the TV advertisement blaring out a timely question to millions across America. I threw my slipper at the off button and missed by a mile—the story of my life.

"Time to get up, Mandy!" I yelled, for what seemed like the millionth time. Mandy was a sweet, loving, four-year-old with the disposition of a sour pickle in the morning. Each day we went through what I called "the ritual." Mandy would wake, slow, pokey, sometimes sullen. She needed my constant prodding, bribes, and jokes to get her in gear. After at least an hour of torturing both of us, she would be her sunshiny self.

Each morning we went through the same little routine. I should have put my foot down, made her shape up, but we had too many obstacles to overcome at the time. I was still in the middle of a nasty divorce from her alcoholic father and could count on fighting with him at least twice a week over jobs, money, visitation rights, and anything else under the moon. So I gave into my daughter's stubborn ways, and she pushed all my buttons. It became our way to start the day

Then there was the issue of my new job, working with an all-man crew driving trucks for the town barn in the lovely little borough of Makingdo, Vermont. I could only wonder how the town had gotten its name, but somehow it seemed fitting for the majority of the people living in it, myself included.

My new job was a spin-off from my old part-time job as a bus driver, only now, instead of being able to spend time with Mandy, I had to work full time. I needed health insurance benefits for the two of us, had to pay the mortgage, support two dogs, a stray cat, and a shitty old Toyota SR5 that I loved for the sunroof and good gas mileage but hated the fact that at least once a month I was sinking money into it.

Three weeks before I had been sitting on my kitchen floor crying into the phone to my friend Kelly. I had been fired from my part-time job at the Table Company after just four months.

"I've never been fired before in my life! I wailed.

The condescending boss had called me into his office. "We are letting you go," he said. "You just aren't working out." I was stunned. Half the people that worked at the Table Company ran out to snort crack or gulp nips on their ten-minute breaks. They were what I called Makingdo's finest or benchies because they always hung out on benches on Main Street looking for dope deals and trouble.

"Oh, it's not you personally," Kelly said.

"Whaaat?" I stammered, trying to focus on Kelly's reply

"Yeah, you must have been ready to get your nickel raise, so he let you go," Kelly said. "They do that to everyone; have for years. That's why just about everyone in town has worked there at one time or another."

"Well, I guess that makes me feel a little better," I said sniffling. "But now, what am I going to do?"

"Something better will come up," she said consolingly. She was right. The very next day I received a notice in the mail to report on September first to the town barn for a full-time position.

Months ago, my uncle Ralph had talked me into applying for the job. "They're hiring minorities right now and you being a woman fits the package," he said over and over.

Somehow that didn't make me feel exactly special but I did as he told me. Lo and behold, nine months of sleepless nights and endless nail chewing months later, I had birthed a good paying job.

Now I had medical insurance, a full-time job, and a never-ending clown of a car. But it was a light at the end of the tunnel of how to pay bills and keep us afloat. Of course, with the good, there was always some bad to balance out — the ying and yang and all that jazz. It meant having less time for Mandy when I felt she needed me most. I had to find someone to watch her after school until I picked her up at almost 5 o'clock. In the winter, it was already dark by then. It seemed that I sent her into the doom and gloom of the morning then saw her again in the cold dusky evening. I looked forward to weekends of us sleeping in snuggled together. I loved holding her cuddled next to me on the couch watching kid's movies late into the night. Her golden hair spilled across the crook of my arm, making me want to see her sleep and to capture the moment forever.

Sometimes at night I would toss and turn, thinking about how much I wanted to take her to museums, and picnics, or out to lunch. If I could, I'd find time to read books and poetry to her, and I wanted her to have at least one magical birthday party. I dreamt of Mandy having tea parties, nature hikes, and special movie nights, many of the things I would have loved to do as a child.

Then there were the nights that I suffered the what-ifs and the maybes. Perhaps I should have watched the clouds more closely, discovered more rainbows, enjoyed more sunsets, smiled more, hugged people more. If I could do it over again, I would constantly chew gum, work as a lumberjack, join the Peace Corps, go on a religious retreat, strand myself on a tropical island, and be a veterinarian and then later an archeologist. But I guess in the end being Mandy's mom was what I was meant to do. I would remember that I can't be who I am not and hoped that the job of being a good mother was something I could strive for until the end of my days.

The tedious drudgery of my job, day in and day out, would get to me. I'd invite Kelly over to vent my problems. It would be one of those nights when my mind would race, and I'd review every bad or sad thing that ever happened to me, starting almost from birth. It would usually end up with the marriage and divorce from Mandy's loser of a father, but in the end, I always realized that I wouldn't change a minute of the pain or disillusionment because, after all, I had ended up being Mandy's mom. Who could ask for more than that? After an exhausting night of lying awake, I would fall into a deep sleep for a few hours until the damn alarm clock buzzed my brains out at 5:30 and I would start it all over again.

On days when I wasn't tired or felt that I hadn't spent much quality time with Mandy, we would play a game called the 'I don't love you' game. First Mandy would say to me as convincingly as she could, trying to look stern and sad all at the same time, "I don't love you!"

Her blue eyes would be sparkling, and I would look at her straight on and say it back to her. Sometimes it would be a standoff for at least a half a minute but whoever laughed first was the loser because we knew it was ludicrous and that of course, we loved each other we thought as we collapsed giggling like crazy into each other's arms.

Mandy watched a cartoon, My Pretty Pony probably more times than the producer who made it. When she wasn't absorbed in the pony show, she would have little fashion shows; constantly changing dresses, even wearing sundresses around the house in the winter and like a true diva leaving a river of clothes behind her that trailed from room to room. Friends often gave me hand-me-downs from their daughters which I gladly accepted. Mandy never seemed to know the difference as long as she had an assortment to choose from.

I couldn't decide if she was aspiring to be a model or if she was just looking for attention which I often felt I didn't have a lot of to give. Her other quest was inventing all sorts of outfits for her few Barbie dolls and sometimes even something for poor old Ken to wear.

She followed a strong and steady regimen of being a very picky eater and consumed so many cans of Campbell's chicken and rice soup that she should have had stock in the company. To make our little two people family dinners more festive — well, as festive as you can get with canned soup, a tired mom, and a feisty child — I would light a candle, use pretty place mats, and even set a few teddy bears around the table using the old adage the more, the merrier. At least three evenings a week, I would try to spend at least a half hour reading stories to Mandy. She loved books and stories that I made up. I used different voices and expressions to keep her entertained. We went to the library for free books every Saturday morning after going to the dump.

The years plodded on, sometimes sweeping by, other times slowly cranking out one obstacle after another. I did eventually get an almost new car, one good on gas that also ran well. I made Mandy pose in front of the little blue Geo Tracker for pictures because we were so proud to have that tiny, shiny car.

For Mandy's ninth birthday I had her invite some of her classmates and her best friend Ally to come to the house in fancy dress-up clothes and hats and to bring their porcelain dolls. I managed to buy one decked out in a pale blue Victorian dress for Mandy, for ten dollars at the local Ocean State Job Lot store. It had blue eyes and blonde braids and looked a bit like her. I made tiny tea sandwiches cut into shapes with cookie cutters; they consisted of peanut butter and jelly and bologna and cheese, all stuff Mandy had requested. I served the girls real raspberry tea with sugar cubes and wore white gloves I found at a thrift shop. The tea was served in a pink and white flowered teapot with flowered paper napkins. They loved the fresh strawberries dipped in brown sugar. It was a delightful day, and it ended with the girls eating cake and playing all afternoon with their dolls. I wished for it never to end; it was as magical for me as it was for them. That night the "I don't love you game" lasted extra long with lots of tickling and hugs. I later fell asleep wondering if Mandy would remember this day that I had tried to make so special.

At last, Mandy made it through high school, with me cheering her on all the way. Mandy had worked hard and eagerly awaited her first week of college.

Kelly and I lounged in Mandy's room, sorting through old boxes of stuff that Mandy left behind. I was so happy to know that Mandy could get an education that I never had but I couldn't face packing and sorting through her stuff alone.

"I'm trying to deal with my impending empty nest, knowing our special times together will soon be a closed chapter of our lives when she heads into the adult world," I told Kelly. Hearing my voice thick with tears, my old buddy was there for me once more. She knew exactly what I was going through as she had said goodbye to her college-bound twins three years earlier.

"Aren't you glad I brought over this bottle of wine, Mama Hen?" Kelly said, pouring me another glass.

"Thanks, you're the best," I said sniffing into my handkerchief.

We were three-quarters of the large bottle of wine gone and laughing at old pictures with crazy hair-dos and outfits. We had a pile of stuff that Mandy would definitely want, but most of it was slated for the trash or the Goodwill box. "Yikes," I said. "She kept her report cards and little stories she wrote in her freshman year, and I thought I was the only packrat."

"Here's to sentimental slobs," Kelly said topping off our glasses. It was good to have an old friend that could make me smile. Under a pile of old cards and newspaper clippings about school events, I pulled out a two-page manuscript labeled creative writing - grade nine. I sank to the floor and started to read it.

Mandy Mason

Grade 9

Creative Writing

Three Golden Balls

We were on our way home it was getting close to dusk. The sky was turning and swirling different colors, of rich purples and red-oranges. The sun was huge like in the movies; it looked blood red and fiery. It looked like whenever it reached the tops of the mountains the trees would burst into flames.

My mother pointed out the sun to me-"look, Mandy, isn't it beautiful?"

My eyes followed her hand and I saw this orange blazing ball sinking behind the mountains. She pulled over on the road to a lookout spot. The cliff peeked out over fields onto a winding stream that looked to me like a silvery snake. Way in the distance was the hills and the melting flame of the sun.

We got out of our car and sat on the hood. It was cool outside, and it was getting close to autumn.

She started telling me a story, telling me to continue looking at the melting sun. My mother loved to read, write poetry and most of all to tell me stories. It was the first time I had ever heard the story. It was about a princess, a frog, and three golden balls and how she lost them. The princess loved the present her father the King had given her (the golden balls). Each time the princess lost the balls into a pool of water the frog would faithfully return them to the princess, always asking for something in return. Until one night, when his request was to be kissed by the princess. The princess did as she had promised, and the frog turned into a prince. Because she had been so kind to the frog and had always kept her word, the prince loved her and they were married.

The sun set was over by the end of the story. The golden ball was lost again, and the frog would find it and bring it back to me my mother told me. So I waited to see if the frog prince would come and return the sun to me the next day, and to see what I would have to give in return.

The next day the sun came out and I barely remembered the story from the night before. I only remembered having a lovely night with my mother, and now that I'm older I've heard this story many times and in many ways but, never as beautifully told as the day the sun was setting and my mom pulled the car over to tell me a tale.

Since then the frog prince has faithfully returned the sun to me, not every day, but when I need the sun's light the most… it's there…my mom.

"Oh Kelly, I never knew she wrote this," I said as tears streamed down my face. "I remember telling her this story when she was about eight."

Kelly had been reading behind me and sounded all choked up as she hugged me. "You done good kiddo," she said hugging me. "You done real good."

MOTHER'S FAVORITE
Clare Kirkwood

She made we sisters matching outfits
coltish girls wore red calico
mutton-sleeved dresses
with black velvet trimmed empire waists

Hounds tooth capes matching skirts and tams
"mod" identical mail order
Campbell Soup paper dresses
cost a dollar and ten soup labels

Mom told each one in private
"You are my favorite" I believed
like God she made me feel
I *was* her favorite

Sister demanded fifty dollar prom gown
sales women bowed to her enchanting beauty
I made my gown for six dollars
knowing our family couldn't afford more

Mom gifted sister the perfect estate ring
she expected no less
broken Claddagh ring came my way
now refurbished a cherished heirloom

Years came and sped by
I was there after Mom fell
we went to the doctor
then we had coffee and fun

As time went by
after Mom's car accident
we went to the doctor
then we had coffee and fun

When sister suddenly
dropped Mom off
I cried, "She's not the same
then we had coffee and fun

More years went by
Mom went to the nursing home
I wept inconsolably
still we had coffee and fun
Over the years I wondered
where my sister was
reflecting now I know
I WAS Mom's favorite

MUD SEASON
bg Thurston

Again spring arrives, uninvited
visitor, arms full of flowers, showy
and short-lived. No matter the rain,
we walk these woods. These paths,
we understand—counter-
clockwise and color-coded.
This season of mud sucks
at the dogs' paws as they pull me
down root-laced trails. Unseen
crows are raising a ruckus,
the forest fills with their caucus
of complaint. Nearby, ominous
creaking—a white pine ready to let go
of the air. I pause, wishing
to witness this end, to hear its fall.
This winter I have lost
three earrings here
and it comforts me to know that
they will remain.
I'm learning how to let go
of everything I love. As far as I can see,
we leave this life with nothing
and I want to be ready.

SECRETS BURIED
Mary Owen

It was one of those life-changing instants. Even now, these sixty years later, my memory retrieves the visual image of that moment. It is accompanied by a sinking feeling, the residue from that conversation with my mother so long ago. As a seven-year-old, I heard what, until that split second was an unthinkable, unbelievable fact from mother. She painstakingly told me, "No honey, the word, 'adopted' means you were not born out of my tummy but from another lady's." Oddly enough, I don't recall the conversation precipitating this shocking revelation.

Thus was my introduction and subsequent formation of a life-long relationship with the deeply kept secrets of adoption. Oh, there were tiny glimpses through the years of the truth of my origins, but those mysteries were guarded, whether intended or perhaps unknown, by my parents. Later, I found the hints or partial truths to be markers along the path to a fuller understanding of my ancestry.

As I grew older, I became sensitive to the pain in the faces of my parents when the subject of my birth came up. My interpretation of their responses to any questions suggested to me that the subject of adoption was taboo. In fact, when the subject was broached by anyone, even as a child feelings of shame and guilt bubbled into my very being. I seemed to carry an obligatory allegiance to the people who so gallantly took me in as a three-month-old baby and raised me as their own. Any question about my birth parents appeared to be a competitive element of discomfort and dishonor to those who were nurturing and parenting me.

As I matured, I lived with the secret and acted as if I were one of them, "them" being my adopted family. Nevertheless, into my adult years I felt that I belonged to no one, and nowhere. Once, I considered joining my maternal family's Scottish clan organization. I was startled to realize I didn't have the bloodline to do that. I felt as if I were a poser, using a borrowed heritage all these years. "Who am I, for real?" I often wondered. Identity confusion of the genetic sort reigned in my life.

Oh, I had a good enough childhood. My parents did the best they knew how. I wanted for nothing. But, there was always a missing element in the relationship, especially with my adoptive mother. I felt I could never please her, yet I owed her so much. After all, she chose me as her own and took care of me to adulthood.

My suspicions about that missing element were confirmed when I was about twenty years old. I was home in Seattle visiting my family after having moved to Massachusetts a year earlier. We were having a lovely lunch with a long-time family friend and peer of my mother's. In the midst of the conversation mother made an illuminating comment to her friend. She was speaking about me as if I wasn't sitting at the table. She said, "You know, there were nights I went to bed and thought, 'I never said a kind word to that girl all day!'"

I thought, "You mean, you knew you were treating me that way and went on doing it anyway?" For my mother to refer to me as "that girl," hit me hard in that moment. As if being referred to in such an impersonal and disconnected manner wasn't bad enough, her admission to her thoughts sent an indication of intentionality that stunned and hurt me. Whether valid or not, that conversation confirmed for me that she didn't see me as an authentic daughter. Although I overcame the initial sting from that comment, I have never forgotten the implications regarding my adoptive status and place in the family.

My sense of loyalty to my adoptive parents was so great, that although I craved to know the information about my origins, any exploration to learn of my biological beginnings and heritage was very limited until after my adopted mother and father died. The State of Washington where I was born and raised was complicit in hiding the deeply held secrets of the biological parents for many adoptees over a certain period of decades. There was a window of years around the 1950's when adoption information was assumed by surrendering parents to be kept sealed from the child forever to protect the biological parents' privacy. In fact, no legal promises were made to keep those records sealed indefinitely. But the customary sealed adoption records protected the surrendering parents from their shame and guilt. So the state held to that practice until it was challenged by people like me. I felt I had a greater birthright to know that information than my birth parents had to keep it from me.

More recently, in the last thirty years or so, Washington State legislators have been struggling over the issue of sealed adoption records. There was one holdout state representative, an adoptive parent who voted against open records. For this person, opening what seemed 'Pandora's Box' was a personal threat. So, one person's objection kept the bill from going forward in the legislature. As a result the secrets of many continued to be held hostage for years. To me, allowing such a stance to continue was a misuse of personal power in a legislative setting. Four years ago, I joined with other adoptees in a grassroots organization to change the law in Washington State. Although it is not an easy process, now adopted people can access their original birth certificates in that state.

It is troubling to me in this arena of sealed adoption records that birth parents have had a greater legal right to hide their identity than the offspring has to know their true heritage. Giving birth seems to have trumped the rights of the individual whose very life is documented at that delivery. In my opinion, the legal system has colluded with parents and promoted social stigmas of shame and guilt for mistakes made decades ago. It is important to take into account that those mistakes' resulted in real people who deserve and I believe have a right, a birthright, to know their entire history, including the identity of their birth parents if they choose.

In fact, the secrets of the adoption of babies, buried over time, create a chasm of hurt and frustration. Issues around family, trust, belonging, abandonment, and self-worth are confused and often result in problematic personality formation and maturation. These issues cannot help but infiltrate difficulties in the personal and relational lives of the adoptees. It seems as if there is an insatiable hole in the heart and soul of an adoptee without answers or closure to the beginnings of their life. With secret after secret, the illegitimacy becomes almost fantasy-like, as if the person was never born. Such secrets for the child abandoned accumulate and are compounded, not only for the child, but as one can imagine, the parent too. Deep secrets develop wounds time does not in itself heal. Rather, the secrets descend to a level of clandestine mystery that doesn't help any party involved.

As it turned out, the State of Washington did change the law, with the caveat that the birth parents had the right of refusal. But if they did not come forward within the first year of the law, then an adoptee could petition to receive the original birth certificate. I waited the required year before requesting my records and was granted my birth certificate. That was a momentous day! Even my postman was excited about the arrival of the document.

I left the Post Office after retrieving my precious letter, driving a short distance to my office. I turned off the engine. Wanting to be alone for this private unveiling, I sat in my car unable to wait another second. With my heart racing and tears streaming down my face, I carefully opened the envelope. It was the document I had never expected to hold in my hands. There in black and white was a copy of my original birth certificate. I knew this was the real birth certificate because it contained information that matched some of the data from my adoption birth certificate.

There was my birth name, something I had always wondered about. And, there it was, the name of my birth mother, a woman whose very womb I had been knit in. It was astounding to me! As wonderful as it was to know this information, it also showed me how much more I didn't know. My birth father's name was not listed and I found later my mother's name had been altered. But, now I had some answers even though they brought more questions. The puzzle pieces were beginning to surface, with the hope that my full story would be revealed. I believe the truth will set one free. Even partial facts can give relief. Honesty, in the end, will provide some solace and peace just through the knowing.

I have only just begun to uncover and explore the factual story of my secret adoption held hostage for so many years. I hope that as time goes on, I will know better who I am and where I came from as I uncover the mysterious hidden truths that have been kept from me so much of my lifetime. Such unveiled knowledge is not just for me, but for my children and grandchildren that they may have a family history and legitimacy that I did not know for so long. To me, the secrets of adoption should be exposed as a birthright for any adult person who desires to know the truth of their existence.

The secrets of adoption have often been born out of the shame and guilt of personal choices resulting in the birth of an unexpected child. Well intentioned birthparents hid the child they bore, by giving that child away to someone else. Then they would often pretend the child never existed. I wonder if one could in fact erase the existence of their flesh and blood child from one's own memory. I believe that in adoption, time's reservoir cannot obliterate the memory of their child no matter how tightly the secret is held. Memory does not forget the secrets of another human held in reserve, however deep they may be buried, or for whatever reason they are kept.

As time marches on, the reservoir of secrets unexposed becomes deeper and more alluring, while at the same time elusive and hopelessly lost to a season gone by. As elated as I have been to obtain my birthright information, my appetite has not been satisfied. I continue to be famished for more facts that tell me who my birthparents were and the story they have to tell me. My journey will continue with faith and hope that I will find more pieces to this illusive story nearly lost in the secrets of time's reservoir.

THE WATER CLOCK
Steve Michaels

Sand is dry
It holds no life
Save scattered bones
some dust mites
I much prefer
A water clock
Each drip is but
A single tock
I keep mine
In the faucet
Best for sleepless nights
It's dripping still
For I refuse
To fix up any pipes

For in the pipes
I keep my dreams
For which I'm biding time
And so I watch
My water clock
As time goes
Slipping by

FAIRY RING
Clare Green

Wooded trees with glowing lights
Fairies offer peace
Silent star beauty

Snowy and slippery road conditions ahead with a steep slope I thought to myself, I had best park the car here on the top of the hill, only a mile and a half from home in Royalston. We'd have to walk home from here. It was winter with a cold, dark and snowy night surrounding us. Luckily, we were well dressed for it.

"Let's get walking, Ned."

"OK."

No flashlight. I was still too young to think of provisioning for one in the car for emergencies, but old enough to be a mother to a seven-year old son. As we emerged from the car, I felt the cold air and sensed the dark moonless evening embrace us. Alone with snowflakes
falling.

I glanced ahead to the surrounding forest and saw a dozen white sparkling lights encircling a small tree close to our parked car. I took comfort from the sight and felt it suggested to me that my son and I would be safe as we walked along the country road toward home. I needed to show courage in this night-time adventure. I silently said a prayer of protection and light for us. Indeed, I was ever thankful for warm winter scarves, wool hats, snow boots, and trusty jackets.

While walking toward home, our mittened hands clasped, we found that our eyes adjusted to the night and realized that we could distinguish the country road and shapes of trees before us. A barred owl hooted from within the woods. We chatted, hummed, and listened to the night sounds as snow swirled around us.

Before too long we passed a familiar neighbor's home and then arrived shortly at ours. It felt good to finally see the golden glowing lights coming from our home. We offered a small prayer of thanks for our safe arrival before we ate supper that night. Warm, fed, and cozy. Home.

It would not be until years later that I would learn about "fairy rings." I immediately realized that was what appeared to us that winter evening: a fairy ring. The quiet celestial presence certainly reassured us as we embarked upon a cold and dark walk that night. Mmm, I thought to myself, a gentle fairy ring, how sweet to bid us comfort—or did we merely intrude upon their woodland evening gathering?

BUDDY DYER'S CAKE
elaine reardon

Buddy Dyer made a cake.
He cut one slice, and
sent me back 30 years.
First I thought about
Auntie Lil's cakes,
my mom's, then mine.
We baked cakes thoughtfully,
considered how we'd frost them—
cooked or buttercream.

When a cake was special,
we added walnuts.
I listened to how Uncle Paul
made my parent's
wedding cake
how my parents saved me
a slice of that cake in a shoebox,
in their attic room.
Mice ate it before I was born.
I wonder if the mice dreamt of their future,
as I was supposed to do.

I was born careless,
and dreamed too much.
Buddy's cake was like
the best part of childhood.
In winter it tasted of summer,
pineapples, black walnuts, and coconut.
White frosting floated over the top like clouds.
He gave me a big slice to take home.

THE OBSERVER
Emily Boughton

I am tortured by the color black. By the chill that runs down my spine, that spreads goosebumps over my skin, and then never lets go. By the overwhelming darkness that inevitably extinguishes any and all sparks of life. The darkness that I can never escape.

That is my task, to meet them in the darkness. I left behind time and the laws of the world to rewind and review their lives until that fateful moment. When the darkness finally claims each one I am there to guide them.

I am not God. Nor am I Death. I am not a Guardian Angel, whatever that may be. I am simply an Observer.

I wasn't always like this. There was once a time when the darkness was just another step I knew would come. I too, long ago, was once human. I walked the Earth, heard my footsteps on the ground and felt the cold wind against my flesh. Almost all of those memories have slipped away from me like rain on a window pane. Now I can only recall flashes. My wife's hair in the moonlight, the smell of her lilac-scented perfume drifting across a room, how her lips felt as they gently touched mine.

When I first met the darkness I was still a young man. The memory of that night glares painfully clear among the rest. It was only a few months after my bride and I had said our vows; the start of our new life in a new town. We had just seen an illusionist perform at the theater. The sun had already set, leaving the oil lit lamps to light our way, their reflections twinkling in puddles left from the day's rain. We started to make our way home and as we turned down an alley, there was a sudden splash and a yowl behind us. I turned away from wife's side for just one second to find a cat furiously hissing at us. I turned back, my wife had stopped, frozen with fear. Panic struck me.

A man stood in front of her, a pistol pointed at her heart. "Please, don't do this," I pleaded with him as I slowly moved in front of my wife, gently nudging her trembling body farther away. She sobbed, her hand reaching out to find mine. I grabbed for my wallet, my watch, anything valuable I had and held it out to him. There was a moment when the gunman and I just looked at each other. "Please just take this and leave," I begged and took a step closer, my hand outstretched. Fear and anger flashed across his face. His hand shook as it clutched the gun in front of him.

I can't remember the pain of the bullet hitting my chest; I only recall lying on the cobblestone as my wife cried out for help. She sat beside me, cradling my head and stroking my hair, salty tears fell onto me. It was not long before I met the darkness. An observer stood there waiting for me to follow.

I was chosen for this task, handpicked by the ones before me. The observer gave me a choice. Either join them and watch over other souls or take the same path as the other humans to a world beyond, where one can finally rest.

I was too young back then to clearly see what I was being offered. I never thought through the consequences. What torture my mind would endure knowing I was going to watch every single person I was assigned die right in front of me. It doesn't matter in what manner they die. Whether it is a slow, peaceful death from old age or the tragic murder of a soul too young to depart, I am always the one who is with them in the end, and in the end, there is nothing I can change. I can only be there to take their hand. I had a choice of seeing Earth again. To see my wife again. Or never returning. I accepted the offer, chose Earth over rest, and became an Observer.

I saw so many other souls before I saw my wife again. It was just a few years to her, but to me it felt as though eons had passed. She walked past a young blonde man I was assigned to. She was wearing a long blue dress and carrying a basket of fresh apples she had just bought from the marketplace. Around her neck she had a simple silver chain with a golden ring. My wedding band. Her long sun-kissed hair was tied back with a silk black ribbon. Even with all the bustling about on the street, people talking and laughing, I could still hear her footsteps on the cobblestone pathway. She seemed happy, as if she was moving on. My heart wrenched.

Forgetting all rules of my order, I stopped watching the young blonde man and desperately tried to call to her. Running to her, calling out her name, pleading hysterically with every ounce of energy I had, every last bit of will, for her to hear me, to see me. But I was nothing more than the wind to her, reduced to no more than a passing shadow, an inkling of what was, invisible to the world. I could stand by her side for decades and she would never notice. No matter how many times I said "I love you" she would never hear me. I crumpled to the ground in my nothingness and she was gone.

I cannot tell you which was more devastating, seeing my wife once again or truly knowing that my humanity was lost.

Many years have passed and times have changed on Earth since that day. The world has grown faster, more rushed. The people more aggressive, but yet also more giving and knowledgeable. Wars have taken soul after soul much too early, and technology has given many souls more time, and I keep observing. There is no sense of reward, nor pain of punishment, I simply am. I watch and wait to guide them.

How odd, that you can go through your existence, and see so many miraculous and horrible things. You could witness the dawn of a new age or the destruction of an entire nation. You could meet a great ruler of a powerful nation or an inventor of a science that saves an entire race. And yet, the simplest of things can make the largest difference.

Her name was Amber. She was a young American girl, just starting off, out from under the wing of her parents, when I was assigned to her. Having recently graduated from studying nursing at a local university, she had hardly a penny to her name.

The first time I observed her, she was walking down the sidewalk of a busy street. It was fall and maple leaves decorated the cold concrete like gold and red splattered paints on a blank canvas. The heels of her short brown leather boots rhythmically clicked as she went on her way. To brace her flesh from the cold brisk winds, she had grabbed a light-weight pea-coat and a purple scarf from her closet that morning. There was a lightness to her steps as she passed the people walking by her, making sure to keep her pace, eager to get to her destination in a timely fashion. She stopped only once to capture a picture with her phone's camera of the sun glistening over a late blooming rose.

I followed her as she turned off the main road and down a quiet, narrow side street lined with quaint little houses all painted in different colors. Each house had its own little yard, a few more manicured than others. Some had festive decorations, ghosts made from old sheets hanging from tree branches, fake gravestones lining the walkways, and signs that read 'BEWARE' next to cobwebbed mail boxes, all already up in the spirit of Halloween.

She walked past the first few houses until she reached the fourth one, number 117. It was an older house, with white clapboard siding, light blue trim, a gravel driveway and old fashioned car port. Years ago it must have looked like a house out of a magazine. With a white picket fence in front of it and some nice green grass, it would be anyone's dream home. Now the paint was slowly chipping off and the wood showing through, but it did not look neglected but rather worn from years of love.

Amber knocked and stepped inside. She took off her jacket and used the elastic band on her wrist to put her long, wavy, dirty blonde hair up in a ponytail as she continued down a hallway into a large sitting room lit by a warn lamp. Beside a small fireplace, its mantel covered with portraits in decorative frames, there were two arm chairs only separated by a small round side table. One of the chairs was empty; occupying the other was an elderly woman. She wore a simple green dress that buttoned down the front and had her fine grey hair tied up in a loose bun.

"Hello, Mrs. Hudson," Amber said sweetly to the woman, "How are you doing today?"

"Hello, my darling. Have you seen Richard?" the woman asked with longing in her voice, "He was supposed to put out the decorations today. The children will be disappointed if he didn't."

Richard was Mrs. Hudson's late husband. I had observed him before he passed on of a sudden heart attack. He was a kind old gentleman with much pride and love in his heart. After serving time as a naval officer he had returned home to finally marry his high school sweetheart. With her help he raised enough money to purchase their own plot of land and build the house that they had always dreamt of. During all the time that I observed him I never saw him be anything but devoted to his family. I remember feeling a bite of jealousy, a nag of envy, for even though he was gone, they'd had so many long years together; broken by age rather than a bullet.

"No, I haven't seen him yet today Mrs. Hudson, but I'll be sure to tell him when I do," Amber replied sweetly, without falter.

"I wonder where he's wandered off to this time," Mrs. Hudson mumbled and shook her head. I could see a stroke of pain hiding deep in her expression, as if her mind was protecting her from the truth, from the loss. I longed for that ignorant bliss.

Amber smiled and stepped into another room, taking out a mop, broom, and dust rag. I watched as she proceeded about her business cleaning, running a load of laundry, and preparing a meal. When Mrs. Hudson was finished eating, Amber assisted her into the bath and after helped her organize a box of old photographs of smiling people. Then she helped her settle into bed and as Mrs. Hudson drifted off to dreams, Amber went up into the attic and took down a box covered in dust. She opened it and pulled out fake cobwebs, plastic gravestones, and a paper skeleton.

Amber arrived home to her apartment later that night after picking up a bag of groceries at the local corner store. The apartment was tucked away just outside the downtown area, connected with three others just like it. The front door led directly into the kitchen, where the scent of vanilla and citrus filled the room. The cupboards and appliances wrapped around one corner while in the corner opposite was a round table with four wooden chairs surrounding it. A hallway led away from the kitchen with two doors on one side, one to a bedroom and the other to a small bathroom. Opposite the doors was an entrance into the living room. It was a small layout but a cozy one. Everywhere against the bland tan walls were little splashes of color, posters, pictures, or other decorations. On the windowsills plants happily sprouted and flowered. Every nook and cranny was filled with love; it was a home.

"Hello, Nate," Amber chirped as she came in and put her keys down on the kitchen counter. Nate was sitting at the kitchen table, bills and bank statements scattered in front of him. He was leaning against the table pulling his long fingers through his short copper hair. In his other hand he twirled a pair of glasses in the air.

"Hello," he said but didn't look up. He was fixated on the pile in front of him. He approached the papers with much distress. Like a thorny bush; every time he reached in, there was nothing good to come out of it.

Amber placed the bag of groceries on the counter; taking off her coat she walked over to him. She leaned over and wrapped her arms around him in an embrace. She gazed at the taunting numbers, "Would you like me to help?"

"No," he said bluntly, almost coldly. She started to pull away but Nate gently grabbed her hand in his and pulled her back, kissing her on the cheek. "Sorry. No, I'm fine. I'm almost done for tonight."

"It's alright, don't worry, I know how much this gets to you. Why don't I make dinner while you finish up?"

"That would be great. What do we have?"

"Well let's see," Amber walked back over to the bag of groceries and then turned to face him with a grin, "Let me surprise you!" Nate raised his eyebrows and smiled before returning to his work. Amber began to take ingredients out of the grocery bags and fridge. As she prepared the meal she gazed out the little window above the kitchen sink. Watching the sun set over the little town she saw the street lights flickering on like sleeping stars. I've always wondered what she was thinking about then. I swear I saw a longing in her eyes.

The next day, after she had finished at Mrs. Hudson's she didn't return to the apartment. Instead she walked to a bar a few streets away. It was only a few lots down from a local sports arena, where small-time teams would compete for bragging rights. As a consequence the losers would always wander in looking to drown their sorrows and the winners would come to celebrate their victory. Tonight was the championship game for the local hockey team.

Amber went in and waved to the bartender, a burly man who looked as though he was already sick of the world even though it was only six at night. She snuck behind the bar and went into the room marked "Employees Only, All Others Keep Out," where she readied herself for her second job. She was greeted by three other girls who were in the process of changing into their uniforms, a plain white t-shirt, black mini skirt and a blue apron that started at their hips.

"Gonna be a long one tonight girls," the oldest one said in raspy voice. I was surprised I hadn't met her yet given the fact that she smelled as though she had bathed in cigarette ashes earlier that morning. There were a few disgruntled moans at the remark "The night's still young," Amber replied with an optimistic smile, "Who knows what it will bring?" The raspy voiced woman shook her head with skepticism as Amber laced up her sneakers, secured her hair in a bun, and began to work.

The older waitress was right, it was a long night. The crowd of drunkards kept growing and the more time progressed the louder it got. Men yelled across the bar about how their team was better than the others while their wives gossiped with each other on the side. There was no rest for the waitresses. They were constantly running back and forth from the bar, to the kitchen, to the tables and booths, sometimes even running into each other.

At a particularly rowdy table sat four men, all of whom had had too many drinks over the course of the night. I grimaced at the sight of them but Amber carried on with as much pep as she could muster. She brought over their order and placed their food down in front of them. She started to grab the empty glasses from the table when she noticed that the last man to receive his food was scowling.

"Is there anything else I can get you?" Amber asked gingerly; she looked tired from running back and forth all night, but nonetheless she managed to smile.

"Yeah, you can get me the right meal!" He blurted at her.

"Is there something wrong, sir?" She asked, pulling out the pad of paper to double check what she had written down. I had heard him give his order to her earlier; she was correct, down to the extra pickles on the side.

"Didn't you hear me, you stupid bitch?" He yelled and took a glass of beer from the table and threw it at her, soaking her to the bone. "This isn't the right order!"

Surprised, Amber lost her grip on the empty glasses and they crashed to the floor shattering at her feet. She didn't retaliate, didn't try to dry herself off. Instead she simply smiled at him and said "I'm sorry about that sir, I'll go fix that right away," and turned from him walking back towards the bar.

As she retreated, her boss yelled to her, "That's coming out of your pay and you better clean it up!" She kept going past the bar and out the back door. Slumping down beside the door, she buried her head in her hands. Beer still dripped off her hair onto her face mixing with tears. I sat down beside her and waited.

When she went home that night the only lights in the apartment were from a small fixture above the kitchen sink and the soft glow of the lamp on Nate's beside table. Amber quietly crept into the bedroom. Nate was sound asleep, his book lying open beside him, glasses crooked on his face. Amber smiled lovingly at him and walked over, picked up the book and dog-eared the page that was open. She took off his glasses placing them beside the lamp and then grabbed a dry change of clothes from the dresser. Before shutting off the light, she leaned over and tenderly kissed him on the forehead.

Amber quietly stepped out of the room and closed the door behind her. She made her way back to the kitchen and grabbed her messenger bag before sitting down at the table. From her bag she pulled out an application for a nursing position at St. Ruth's Hospital. For a while she just looked at it, flipping between the two pages. She sighed and put it back down on the table, rubbing her fingers against her temple. When she finally picked up her pen a gleam of determination sparkled in her eyes. As she filled out the form I felt my heart sink.

On Sunday Amber and Nate had the day off. They slept in late, past noon, and woke up holding each other close. Nate was the first to get up; while Amber stayed in bed a bit longer he prepared chocolate chip pancakes. She finally woke up and wandered into the kitchen, her hair a frizzy mess. He smiled at her and I could tell that no matter what she looked like he would love her. I remembered that feeling. As she sat down at the table he topped her stack of pancakes with a whipped cream smiley face. She giggled as she saw his creation and he sat down across from her with his own stack.

"Let's go on a walk through the trails today," Nate merrily suggested, "We can pack a picnic and watch the sunset over the reservoir."

"That sounds like a fantastic idea," Amber replied with a broad smile, "Let's do it."

That afternoon they walked down the trail with their fingers laced together. The trees had turned to bright oranges, reds, and yellows. Strolling down the trail it was like entering a giant kaleidoscope. They didn't talk much; I got the feeling that they didn't need to, they simply needed to be with each other. It was as if they could look at each other's face and know everything without saying a word.

As they reached the top of the path they had a clear view to the calm water. The sun was just beginning to set, filling the horizon with streaks of purples, pinks, reds even more fantastic than the colors of the trees. Crickets began to serenade them as they lay down on the grass beneath the branches of a great oak tree.

"This is absolutely stunning," Amber said squeezing Nate's hand.

He looked at her and could see the beauty of the world in her eyes.

She rested her head on his shoulder. He turned back to the sky and whispered, "I'm glad you're happy."

Bliss, pure untainted bliss, free of any worries and cares. That is what I witnessed that day. And it tore me apart. For the first time in a long time I felt my heart break, as if I was once again human.

"Stop, please stop!" I cried falling to my knees, "I can't handle this. I can't go any further! Don't make me watch this fall apart." Suddenly the world around me froze. The brilliant colors drained away until everything was grey. I didn't need look up. I knew where I was. The world of the Observers, a world of nothingness. My world. In front of me stood one of my colleagues. The man I first met in the darkness, who laid this path before me. He told me long ago that I had a purity, a joy found in wonder. But he never sees the pain? He looked down at me as I continued to stare at the ground.

"What troubles you?" he asked me.

"You very well know what!" I snarled. Rage swelled inside me like a tsunami but it quickly turned to waves of sorrowful disbelief. "How can you stand by and watch, knowing that each and every happy moment will end in despair, in grief? Knowing that, no matter how much you wish to help there is nothing you can do? What wonder is there in the demise of hope? How can you bear it? What happened to your soul?" He did not answer. I shook my head, "I can't do this anymore. I can't."

"You know as well as I that you must finish what you began, you must continue," he urged, "This is your task, your purpose, you cannot turn away now." I let my eyes meet his. Behind the illusion of numbness I saw a glint of pain, of empathy.

"If we do not do this task than no one will," as he spoke he held out his hand to me. "If we do not guide them, ferry them to their next step, then we abandon humanity. If we stop, all of those souls will be forever lost, wandering in the darkness. We must be there to guide them, to know and remember the truth in their lives."

My gaze drifted back to the empty floor. As if in a dream --- no, a nightmare --- I could see my wife alone. Guideless, she wandered in the darkness that I had met so long ago, no hope of freedom or redemption. Finally I took his hand. As he helped me to my feet he continued, "You were not chosen by chance. You were chosen for this task because you, like the ones before us and the ones after, have a strong heart. You can see the truth in people that others cannot. Your soul was still untainted by the cruelties of the world."

His words seemed to drift through the darkness. I let the thought of my wife, of the souls who would be lost, consume me and guide me. I closed my eyes and drew an empty breath. My gaze returned to a world of color. I was back on the path overlooking the glimmering water with Amber and Nate. A simple ring now decorated her finger and there was still bliss.

The next few weeks were uneventful. Amber and Nate spent Halloween at Mrs. Hudson's dressed in matching costumes, handing out candy to the neighborhood kids. Amber continued working at the bar without incident. Mrs. Hudson kept asking where Richard was. The couple feasted with Amber's family on Thanksgiving and shared the news of their engagement. Through it all I felt numb. Then, as if a reflection of my heart, the first snow came and covered the houses and the trees in a soft sheet of white. The reservoir that had been cascaded by color, froze.

On that day, Amber left Mrs. Hudson's wearing a light coat to brace her skin from the cold. A white scarf wrapped around her neck and she had slipped on a pair of fingerless gloves to match. On her way back home she stopped at the post office. Rubbing her hands together for warmth and stomping the snow off her boots at the door, she walked over and unlocked her post box. There were a few pieces of mail inside. She was about to place them inside her bag when the return address on one piece caught her eye. It was from St. Ruth's Hospital. She paused; surprise danced across her face. She opened the letter as if it were an ancient parchment, fragile and precious. As she scanned the words on the page I saw her face light up with joy. Before she shoved the letters in her bag I caught a glimpse of the word 'Accepted.' Then she took off running for home.

As she ran her boots left footsteps in the snow. She was only a few blocks away from home; she paused at the crosswalk that I watched her cross everyday as she came home from work. She glanced both ways. Excitement filled her vision. She did not see the car barreling around the corner and down the road, slipping on the icy pavement, unable to stop.

The sound of screeching tires. A car horn. Limbs petrified by fear. Flesh against metal. Snow and ice flying into the air. A woman screaming. Scarlet blood staining the once pure snow. The driver running from his car and trying to call to her. Nate, just blocks away, hearing the commotion and dashing to help, not knowing who had been struck. His sobs as he cradled her.

Silence.

As she drew her last breaths the world began to fade. Once again the colors drained until nothing was left but Amber and me. Her eyes flickered open, and for the first time she could see me. I tried to smile but my head bowed solemnly. She stood up bewildered and took a few steps back as the pain of the world left her. Glancing around as if looking for someone, her fingers felt for her ring. Her eyes fell back to me and she watched the tears roll down my cheeks. She opened her mouth to speak but no words came. Her brow furrowed almost pleading.

"I'm sorry," I said in a gentle whisper, though the words hung heavy in the air. Questions ran across her face but she said nothing, just stared back at me. I saw her feel for her ring again as she held her hand close to her heart. I could feel my own fingers searching for the ring that bonded my wife and me together.

"He'll be okay," I knew this in my heart the same way I knew my wife had been okay. "I know it won't be easy, but he will be okay one day and so will you."

A faint troubled smile creep across her lips but it faded quickly. She clutched the ring closer. I extended my hand to her and after a moment's uncertainty she took it.

Together we walked out of the darkness.

MEETING EPONA
elaine reardon

Jess called at supper time
The wood stove crackled heat
from cherry wood and birch
supper was a minute from ready

Jess said he was weaker
wanted me to help him try
alchemical silver injections
I wondered what alchemical
injections were and we talked

No but I'll help you
it may be to heal
it may be to pass
easier—Let me sit with it a while

I filled my plate at the stove
 and placed it on the table
The room shifted
and breathed differently
a whoosh of energy
swept into the room
and then into me
I asked—*Who*

Epona filled me
so I began to sing
I sang out for Jed
on key and strong
I sang for the whole
length of dirt road
steady and strong
I sang for every being
I could think of
I sang for Jess again
one last time.

RESERVOIR OF THE HEART
Steve Michaels

Her arteries were all clogged. The doctors said Maris had about nine months to live.

"Time to make the bucket list," said her sister Lottie, always ready with a crass comment, for humor made the best defensive weapon.

"Isn't this how mom died?" Maris inquired softly.

"Think so," replied Lottie. "Real bitch, ain't it! 'Course, she could have been hit by a bus. You too!"

"Lottie, do you enjoy making this worse?" sighed Maris.

"Who's making it worse? You asked me to go to the doctors with ya. Then they give you that bombshell, and I'm just supposed to duck and cover? I don't think so!"

"Just shut up, Lottie," muttered Maris, holding back tears by starting a fight with her sister. It always worked.

"Excuse me?" challenged Lottie. "If I was you, I'd shut the hell up! You know I don't need this shit right now. I'm trying to finalize my divorce. And the kids are real nasty shits. You know what it's like to live with two hormonal and bitchy teenagers? It sucks. God, Maris! What do you want me to say? We went through all of this with mom; it ain't getting easier you know."

"Fine. Enough then. Call me a cab. I won't trouble you anymore."

"Jesus! Come on. You know, I'm not the comforting type. Why the hell isn't Tom here?"

"I wasn't ready to tell--"

"Screw that Maris! He's your husband. And you don't think he knows. He saw how mom died. Why are you making this difficult?"

"I don't know…"

Maris really didn't know. And neither did Lottie. Perhaps it was her sister's acid tongue that Maris needed, so as to spit at the doctors for giving her this death sentence. But Lottie only used her acerbic wit for putting up fences. Nothing Lottie could say would change the current outcome. What had she been thinking? Lottie was her sister. She had wanted her there because of that tried and true bond. Yes, Tom was her husband. A good man. But not a sister. Not her sister.

"Wait," said Lottie, looking into her sister's large eyeglasses, where the tears were not only present but magnified. "You know, you're a real pain in the ass. I'll take you home. We can tell Tom together. But I'm going to let you do the talking."

Tom was already at home when they arrived. He had taken the day off in fact. Lottie had actually called him. It was a conspiracy! Her sister and husband in cahoots, when all along she had thought them bitter enemies. It seemed to reek of soap opera drama. Especially now that Maris had only one life to live.

Like the sands of an hourglass; oh how the stomach turns! That's what Lottie would have said. Oh Good God! Her sister was in her head now. Maris didn't know if that made things better or worse.

"What did they say?" Tom asked, unsurprisingly agitated. "How much time have we got?"

"All the time in this world," sighed Lottie, lighting a cigarette.

"Be serious," barked Tom; he didn't have the patience to deal with Lottie now or most days.

"Nine months," breathed Maris.

"Nine months? How can they be so specific?" remarked Tom, in disbelief.

"Didn't know my sister came with an expiration date, did ya?" said Lottie, right before a long puff of smoke.

"You shut up!" ordered Tom; their conspiratorial alliance now ended. "Are you sure they said nine months? How can that--"

"Does it matter? That's at the most," Maris stated.

"Right, Yeah, right. At most," exhaled Tom. "So what now?"

"We start living!" exclaimed Lottie, arms stretched high like she was about to launch into a musical number. Which she would have, Maris suspected had she not be seized by a smoke-filled coughing fit.

Tom looked at Lottie with greater contempt. "What do you suggest?" he growled. "Jump out of airplanes? She has a heart condition, you twat!"

"Now don't be that way, Tom," whispered Maris. "She's only trying to--"

"We don't need her help. You have me," muttered Tom above

choked-back tears.

"Oh, she has you all right. By the balls!" cackled Lottie.

"Fuck you!" screamed Tom.

Maris was forced to play referee at many of these matches. She longed for an actual whistle at the moment. This could go on for hours, she thought. And she didn't have many hours left.

"Stop. Just stop! This is my life remember? I need a say in it!"

"You'll have your say, Maris. As long as she stays out of it!" yelped Tom.

"Oooo," cooed Lottie. "How cute! He thinks he's being the tough guy. Oh come on! You have no control over her. You never did. I mean it was kind of us to let you think so, but honestly. Come on, Maris! I see why you called me. Let's go."

"Wait," declared Maris. Her eyes fixed on Tom, who looked like a dog about to be put out of its misery. His bark really was worse than his bite. But he had never barked at her. Only Lottie. And he didn't know how to bite. Lottie and her friends always joked that Tom was whipped. But really he just enjoyed making Maris happy. Only now did Maris feel a bit of regret for allowing him to dote on her all these years. As if she had taken up too much of his precious time.

"Tom," Maris said, after one too many heartbeats. "I love you."

And she left.

. . .

"Where to now, kid?" said Lottie, starting up the car out front. "I'll take you anywhere you want. 'Course, this will be a lot more exciting when my alimony checks start coming in!"

Lottie laughed from behind the wheel. She was now holding the steering mechanism between her knees while trying to light another cigarette. Maris grabbed hold of the wheel out of concern for public safety, not to mention her own, but what did that matter.

"Just once around the block, should suffice," huffed Maris.

The smell of smoke wasn't nearly as choking to her as the last nine hours had been. She breathed in deeply. The smoke of Lottie's cigarette, actually felt like it was calming her down.

"You want one?" offered Lottie, taking back the wheel with her one good hand. "'Course, they say nicotine is a gateway to other drugs. Say, I wonder how long til they put you on morphine. No offense."

Maris took no offense at this point. Instead, she took this opportunity to stare blankly out the window.

"Want me to turn on the radio?" Lottie asked as she instantly pushed in the dial with her wrist. And the car became filled with the disorienting syncopation of an old Zombies' tune that breathlessly muttered on about time and season.

"Oh Jesus! Remember this shit?" coughed Lottie. "Hey forget the morphine! Let's go drop some acid! Ha!"

Lottie's words really were comforting. That was the nice thing about her humor. Her sharp tongue so easily cut through these dark times.

Keep talking Lottie, Maris thought, dance my cares away.

When Lottie was sixteen, she thought she was pregnant.

"God Damnit! I'm about to become an afterschool special here, Maris," she screeched while Maris held the pregnancy test in her unsteady hands.

They were in the bedroom they shared. Being only eleven months apart, they were forced to share just about everything. Secrets were no exception.

"What the fuck does it say?" barked Lottie, from her bedside, the agitation caught in her throat.

"Hold on," puffed Maris, nervously. "I need to check the instructions again."

Maris stared blankly at the carton. Her eyes went back and forth from the stick to the tiny black print on the side of the box. And then back again.

"Jesus, Maris! Just give it to me straight," howled Lottie.

"It's negative," said Maris; her voice went up a slight octave.

"Christ! Just give me the damn thing," vented Lottie, as she grabbed ferociously for the stick in Maris' sweaty palms.

She held it up to the light.

"Thank fucking God!" Lottie proclaimed. "I thought for sure I was dead."

. . .

"You know for a lazy ass shit at least he loves you. I mean, we all bust his balls, but you don't find love like that much places."

True to form, Lottie had kept talking and making jokes all throughout the drive. And despite all the expletives, every other word was marked by genuine fool's wisdom.

"Hey, if I wasn't about to get half of Brad's money in the divorce, I'd Thelma-and-Louise our asses off the road. 'Course, I really don't want those two little shits to have it all, so I won't!"

"Were you ever happy, Lottie?" sighed Maris, not just in frustration, but in deep empathy as well.

"Yeah, once or twice, I guess. Like the actual day I got married. I do love a party. And it was all about me. So glad I chose you for a maid-of-honor! You know Christine actually slept with the best man? Talk about cliché! 'Course she does have two kids now. Wonder if she ever told Don one of them was his...

"And then when the kids were born. Labor hurt like a mother, but the doctors were right. You block it all out, and there they are. God, Margaret is just like me. Must be why I hate her so much. Did you want kids, Maris?"

"I did, once," murmured Maris. "But that would have made this all harder. I mean, I don't think there would be enough room for any kids in my choked heart."

"Fuck! That's some deep shit, Sis. Maybe we should all have these near-death experiences. Make us better people, you know. . ."

They arrived back to the house about ninety minutes from when they left.

"I'm sorry for being such a twat," said Lottie, smiling through the open door of the car.

"Whatever you do, don't tell Tom he was right! We like him docile, remember?"

"I won't," promised Maris. "Love you."

"No one more, kid," breathed Lottie, holding back her smoker's cough until she drove away.

Maris approached the door to her and Tom's house.

Should I run to the door? she thought. Am I wasting too much time already?

She quickened her pace a little, unsure of what kinds of activities would make her condition worse at this point. Everything the doctors said after giving her the time of death was just like it happens in the movies. There were echoing and incoherent ramblings. The floor slid away as if to swallow her. And then all was frozen.

Time really does stand still, thought Maris, thinking back on the day's events.

She would tarry no longer.

Opening the door quietly, she considered just packing a bag. She had put Tom through enough today. For a lifetime. She would stay at Lottie's. Call her back. Stay with her a few days. But why?

"Tom," she called firmly in the doorway. "I'm back."

"Jesus, Maris! How could you take off--?"

"Don't yell, Tom!" Maris declared, stronger than she could ever muster.

"I know...I know," replied Tom, lowering his tone and stammering for lack of control over the situation. "It's just, how could, I mean, I'm sorry, but, you can't just, you know…"

"I know…"

Silence entered the room. Maris longed for Lottie to come charging in, to fill the space with a sarcastic or inappropriate comment. Then, "You can go with Lottie...if you want. I mean, she makes you happy. I try to...I thought I was strong enough--"

"You are." cried Maris. "You are! You are the strongest man I have ever known. Please. Don't go thinking otherwise. I didn't agree with Lottie, you know that. I was simply keeping the peace, as I have always done. I'm sorry I won't be around to do that anymore, but she isn't your sister. You don't owe her anything. And we can blame it all on the disease! I don't know why it couldn't spare me...I don't know why it chose me."

"Well, it's probably because it couldn't kill Lottie," remarked Tom, with a sudden and non-lethal grin. "I mean, nothing could."

Then they laughed. Together.

"Is it silly to ask," began Tom, the sadness creeping in again, "why this is happening to us?"

"I think--I think we have to stop asking so many questions. We both know how hard this will be to accept, but, let's face it, we only have a matter of time."

The silence returned. But now it was comforting and filled with the love of just two people.

Her arteries were full. She knew that now. But it wasn't just the disease. Her life had given her so much and a lot to deal with. She was filled, though, with compassion for all those around her. Tom and Lottie especially. At this very moment, she was the closest she had ever been to both of them at the same time. For the heart has multiple chambers. And despite them being sealed off at times by an allegiance to one or the other, she understood that for now, all four channels were open. Her heart became flooded. And knowing that, her heart could just burst.

THE TEACUP
Bonnie Arnot

Harold cut the blueberry bread he had taken out of the freezer before bed last night and set the not quite even slices on the fading violet design covering Irene's serving plate. He added mugs, Irene's fancier teacup, and a bowl of lemon wedges to a tray and carried everything out to the screened-in porch.

"I used the last of the frozen berries for these," Irene had said as she double-wrapped one of the loaves to prevent freezer burn.

Harold, never Harry to her, had patted her hand. "Fresh'll be ready in a couple weeks."

He had harvested the first picking of their forty-year-old berry bush in the backyard by himself and wondered at his impatience. The chore never seemed like drudgery when Irene worked beside him. He remembered to place the berries single-layer on a pan in the freezer before jumbling them into bags. That would please her.

He knew Irene didn't mind the kids picking her up from the hospital instead of him. His gnarled length folded less easily behind the wheel these days, though he had at first balked when Irene suggested that she do most of the daytime driving.

"We're a team," she said. "You have better night vision."

Teamwork, Harold accepted, was the saving grace of their senior years. He set the mugs around the table he'd handmade to fit the porch corner. A light drizzle fell, but after four days of staring at hospital walls, Irene would appreciate being outside. Still, he knew her hands would be achy, something she would try to remedy by stretching her fingers down beside her porch rocker, back and forth, curl and straighten. Harold would wordlessly hold his hand out and know exactly how hers would fit in the curve of his palm as he kneaded the pain away.

Too soon to steep the tea, he sat a moment in his rocker and cradled Irene's china teacup, etched on the outside with silver pagodas and pine trees, part of a set he'd bought for her while on shore leave in Japan during his five-year world tour in the Navy. Those years apart—visits home had rarely been granted—almost lost him, Irene. At first, he received a letter every week.

"The town council added two benches to the park," she wrote. "My sister Nancy got engaged and asked me to be her maid of honor."

Harold wrote about the countries where the ship anchored and sketchy details of his life as a mechanic. Only so many interesting things could be said about running machinery that turned salt water into fresh, though he took pride in his efficiency record.

Irene's treasured letters started to dwindle, and Harold told himself that she was planning her sister's bridal shower and helping with wedding details. When one letter said, "I am going to the wedding with my brother," Harold read Irene's loneliness between the lines.

It took a large chunk of his saved pay to send Irene the china set. The accompanying letter told her he kept one of the cups that had a lady's face molded into the bottom of the interior. "It comforts me every night to look into this cup and picture your eyes, your smile."

Harold never regretted the expense. The letters again arrived every week and he and Irene married two months after his return. The only nights they had spent apart had been when they had their three kids and during this hospital stay necessary for Irene to recover from pneumonia.

Harold's phone pinged and the text read that the kids and Irene were five minutes away. He hauled himself up from the rocker and returned to the kitchen to pour steaming water into the readied teapot. He breathed in the familiar Earl Grey and carried the teapot out to the porch. He once again picked up Irene's teacup. A fine crackling in the delicate veneer lined the lady's still beautiful face.

"Yeah, the old girl's held up just fine." A car pulled into the drive. Harold opened an umbrella and went out to welcome Irene home.

THE YOUNGEST ONE
Clare Kirkwood

(Remember when—birthday poem for Bill)

He was patient and content
the best a baby could be
a gift for a busy mom
who now had three

Mother's girls were a handful
running near but mostly far
Bill was happy with
a sandbox full of cars

He was the precious apple
of our aging parents' eyes
He's still my baby brother
though now a bit more wise

He was truly wonderful
to the animals in our care
Loving them more tenderly
than other children dared

There's a picture of a VW sand castle
Bill was proud to "drive"
at a park in Warwick Cousin Mark
crafted while still alive

Visiting the neighbor's dairy barn
could get stinky smelly
So much fun to tickle Bill
blowing raspberries on his belly

We were sore amazed
and soon began to shout
teaching him baseball
behind our country house

I taught him how to
turn and bat to right
When he turned to left
and hit it out of sight!

Amazing a child knows
exactly what to do
He was ambidextrous
So we learned it too

Once when Dad n' Bill went
out for an ice cream date
Bill was asked to keep it quiet
as they came back home late

"We DIDN'T have ice cream!"
"DAD!!" I cried as I pulled a face

We did some autumn haying
with friends living nearby
using the double cab pickup
traversing verdant hills on high

He was my Edgartown hero
when we got the boot

No place to sleep except
illegal beaches it's true
Our family left us
In a right nasty snafu

Bill's quick thinking and actions
got us through the night
Our mosquito pocked bodies
gave us all quite a fright

Life was far from easy then
we had our heartaches true
life back then was simpler
and richer than we knew

Riding pigs, making snow forts

jumping in the leaves
fishing, catching frogs
running in the fields

Dune buggies, motorcycles
VWs and the rest
jumping from the hayloft
really was the best

Sliding down the front lawn
to get on board the bus
making friends and enemies
learning how to cuss

Bill don't forget you are
amazing, intelligent and kind
you are a gentle hard-working man
with a brilliant creative mind

Take what you need in life
and gently shrug the rest
remember one thing always
I know you are the best!

WHERE WOULD I BE WITHOUT MY SHADOW?
Diane Kane

His real name was Henry Bennett, but everyone called him Shadow. He lived in a two bedroom single wide trailer with his wife Charlotte and his daughter Debbie. It wasn't easy for him to make ends meet, yet Shadow would share everything he had with anyone in need. At thirteen years old, when I became best friends with his daughter, I was a troubled teen from a turbulent home. He opened his door and heart to me. Shadow was my hero.

As a confused teen, I often made poor decisions. Like the time Shadow and Charlotte had gone away for the day with friends. I thought it would be a good idea for Debbie and me to take Shadow's car for a ride. Not having a license seemed like a minor detail but the police took it seriously. Luckily, they knew Shadow and left the discipline to him.

"Diane," he said with a stern face. "What were you thinking?"

"We were only practicing driving on the dirt road," I explained.

"Tell you what," he said. "Let's leave the driving to me at least until you get your learners permit."

He let me off easy on that incident. There would be many other times I tested his patience and love. Both held steady.

From the day she was born, Debbie was the sunshine of Shadow's life. When she was twenty, the unthinkable happened; Debbie died in a car accident. I wasn't in the car but felt responsible because I wasn't there to save her. Not only had I lost my best friend, I thought I had lost the love of her parents as well. That day when I walked into the trailer, my heart pounded in my chest, and my legs trembled. Shadow sat on the couch surrounded by family and friends trying to console him.

"I'm so sorry Shadow," I said as I stood unsure in the doorway.

He ran to the door and hugged me like he never wanted to let me go.

After all the services were over, everyone went home. Shadow packed up his lunchbox and his broken heart and went back to work. I stayed with Charlotte and took her for rides every day. I couldn't think of anything I could do for Shadow.

Over the years I stayed close. It was hard to watch Shadow and Charlotte grow old without Debbie. Shadow became sick and could no longer work. During one of my visits, they told me their car had broken beyond repair. They couldn't afford another. I was married, and my husband Tom worked on cars. We happened to have an AMC Eagle, a solid old clunker that Tom had fixed up. We told them they could use it for as long as they needed it.

"This car drives just like a Cadillac," Shadow said with a smile. When he drove up the road sitting so high and proud, it looked like a Cadillac.

A few years later, when Charlotte passed away, Shadow was lost. He would come to our house for dinner on Saturdays, but I knew that wasn't enough.

"Shadow, why don't you stay overnight?" I asked. "Our pets like your attention and Tom needs you to help him cheer on his sports teams."

"I could try it," he said, and soon it became a cherished weekly ritual.

Shadow always loved children. After he had retired from the railroad, his part-time job as a crossing guard was the highlight of his days. On holidays he would dress up and give out candy. One year just before Christmas he fell and broke his ankle. He wasn't able to work for three months. The saddest part for him was not playing Santa for all the kids at the bus crossing. My friend sold costumes, and when I told her, she had a perfect idea.

"Well, who do we have here?" he smiled when we came to his door in our costumes.

"It's just Mrs. Claus and an elf looking for Santa," I said.

We helped Shadow into a plush red suit and wheeled him a half-mile to his crossing corner with a bag full of candy. I never saw a happier Santa.

The next year, when Shadow fell and broke his hip, the doctors said he would have to go to a nursing home. But his sister Barbara and I thought differently. With our help, Shadow stayed in his handicapped apartment. His sister brought him lunch and visited with him during the day. After work, I brought him dinner, and we would watch his favorite television shows.

I took days off to take him to his doctor appointments. On the way home, we would stop at the supermarket. I would help him into the wheelchair once again and push it around.

"Do you think we could stop at the department store?" he asked, and my back would twitch.

It was hard for me to get the wheelchair in and out of the trunk of my car a third time but I could never say no. I would see him struggle in silence, to boost himself in and out of the chair. I knew I had no reason to complain.

Eventually, Shadow went to the hospital with congestive heart failure.

"The fluid will need to be removed monthly by paracentesis," the doctor said. "The nearest hospital that can do that procedure is fifty miles away."

I took him. After a few months, he needed to go twice a month and not long after that, once a week. On the long ride, we would share laughs over old stories. One of his favorites was about me taking his car for a ride down the dirt road. Shadow always wore his signature black cowboy hat and a big smile. Everyone at the hospital got to know him.

"How's it going, cowboy?" the valet in the hospital parking lot asked as he helped me get Shadow into his wheelchair.

"I'm doing fine, but my horse was a little lame this morning, so we left her in the barn."

When I sat next to Shadow in his hospital bed, knowing I wouldn't see him much longer, he said to me, "Diane, I owe you so much."

"What are you talking about?" I said. "I owe you. You took me in when I was a kid. You fed me and made sure I was safe—and you put up with all my trouble."

"Ahh, you were no trouble."

"Shadow, that's why I love you so much."

"Why's that?"

"Because you've always loved me unconditionally."

I don't know where I would have ended up without Shadow. This humble man had given me so much. Shadow taught me that the best presents are not the ones you hold in your hand. The greatest gifts are the ones you hold in your heart.

EPIPHANY
bg Thurston

the soul of the commonest object
seems to us radiant –James Joyce

Coffee poured into blue speckled mugs,
birds gathering outside the kitchen window,
the steady procession of black-capped
chickadees darting to the feeder
while a queue of nuthatches and titmice
line the lilac's brown branches.

And the red squirrel's antics, as he
tightropes across the snowy porch rail
outwitting the young dog yet again
such bravado should be admired
for its fearless finesse. The flag
that salutes the slight breeze,
its stripes forever rippling
the colors of blood and freedom

At every instant, the present
weaves together with all of history
to become mostly forgotten.
So today, look, really look
into the kind eyes of the person
with whom you have spent half a life,
three decades of waking up
eating dinner, walking together
into the future with nothing

but an invisible constellation
to guide you. And realize that
what has been will not always be,
as you face each other, the tiger cat
purring and looping figure-eights
around your snug, slippered feet.

TIME AND ROSE MARIE
Steve Michaels

Sometimes I actually envied her, even though her mind was not as it was. It was strange to see her going backward and being locked in time, like something out of a science fiction movie. Some days she seemed as though she was on a repetitive loop, stuck in the moments of long ago. Yet her ability to conjure up past acquaintances and kin due to resemblances in faces was somewhat magical. And it often was like reliving the past daily.

"I haven't finished putting up the wallpaper yet! The dining room is such a mess! Never be ready in time for the holidays at this rate."

"What the hell is she talking about, Dad?" asked Duncan, our youngest, rather exasperated from spending this little amount of time with her. He was thirty-three. Our youngest and a bit of surprise for both of us.

"Leonard! Oh, Leonard! Whatever you do, don't look at it! You'll hate it, and I don't want to hear it from you right now," Rose Marie shouted at him.

"It's all right," I said calmly to both of them. "Leonard was just leaving."

I ushered Duncan out, all the while pretending he was Rose Marie's long-dead brother. Duncan, much too frustrated to play along, wrenched his elbow from my grasp and headed out of the room ahead of me.

"This is bullshit!" he exploded. "You asked me to come see her, even though you know how much is going on with my work. You said it would be good for her, but I'm Uncle Leonard? And I'm pretty sure she hated the guy! What's with you, Dad? Who do you enjoy torturing more, her or me?"

Duncan was staring at me with great contempt. It was like he was sixteen all over again, and I was refusing to let him borrow the car. I held back a smile at this. Then finally, I said, sternly but softly, "No. No. I don't like torturing her...or you, but she's still your mother."

"That," he enunciated with frothy loathing, pointing a shaky, yet derogatory finger at Rose Marie in the other room, "is not my mother!"

He turned then and left, slamming the door for melodramatic emphasis. I could have made him stay and argued with him, but he wasn't all that off. She was not acting like his mother. This was Rose Marie from before he was born. When she and I were newly married. And at that time, every action and word was made in self-defense of the choices we were making. Duncan, still a bachelor, didn't understand how young married couples must sometimes divorce themselves from their families to begin their lives anew. And it wouldn't have helped if I told him how much I hated his Uncle Leonard, who was a real bully. Never a nice thing to say to Rose Marie or myself. So much like their father; critical and tyrannical. Both men abhorred Rose Marie's life choices. I was no exception. They both considered me a weak man, but as I saw it, she didn't need any more chauvinists in her life. I can't imagine what it must feel like to have two overbearing fathers in your life. And I suppose having to contend with such strong minds, must weaken one's own.

They say Alzheimer's is hereditary. And I suppose someone in the family may have had it, at some point, at some time. It didn't really matter. Growing up, my parents would refer to it as Old Timer's or dementia. As such, I may not have really known what it was until Rose Marie was diagnosed with it. And even then I didn't fully understand what it was or what it was going to do her, to us, to our family.

It happened slowly. Having read a few articles in Reader's Digest and spoken to doctors, everything was all very typical. It started with the misplaced items. Forgetting appointments. Running late because she wouldn't admit she forgot about the appointments. In retrospect, the whole thing was classic, textbook, and annoyingly cliché. All these signs and my growing understanding through various texts and pamphlets, upon actual diagnosis, should have prepared me for her new manner of misinterpreting names and faces. And at times it was even amusing.

She once thought the UPS man was an old lover come to call. I meant to beat her to the door as she was growing more unpredictable of late. I was off in another room upstairs, when I heard the doorbell. And so I stood at the top of the stairs as she opened the door. She was instantly taken aback.

"Harry!" she gasped. "What are you doing here? I'm married now. What if Todd should see you?"

The delivery man looked dazed and confused, and not because he was young or in college. Obviously, he didn't get the joke.

"What the--" he began.

I swiftly came down the stairs at that moment. Why I had frozen myself in time with her, I don't really know. But I eventually came to this poor man's aid.

On the way down the steps, I flirted with the idea of pointing to a hidden camera in my house and telling him he was to be on television. But I was really torn between laughing and crying. So instead I told him to never mind her, like she was the dog let off her leash. I grabbed the package. He wanted me to sign for it. I hastily scribbled a line that bared no resemblance to any of my signatures past, present, or future. Then I shut the door.

Rose Marie cried.

"He meant nothing to me," she muttered.

I held her and whispered, "I know."

Our daughter Susan had it the worst. Every time she visited, it ended in a screaming fit from her mother.

"Fuck you, mother! Todd and I don't care what you think! And I happen to like working!"

Susan began to cry, which only made my wife sound more vindicated and vindictive.

"That's right! Cry, you bitch! That's what you get for beating me as a child! Now get out! Get out!"

Susan and I retreated outside.

"How can you let her scream at me like that?" she wept as we stood on the porch. "Was grandma really such a bitch? She loved us kids, she never harmed us."

"Of course, she loved you," I told her. "Grandchildren can have a profound affect on people."

"Yeah, but you never beat us! It makes it seem like Grandma Carol was so two-faced," Susan said.

"Well," I began, and I stopped myself from saying the truth, "you didn't know grandma when your mother and I were young."

"Sure, whatever, but I've never seen Mom like this."

"It's the disease. Your mother is trapped in what I like to call her reservoir of time. Don't ask me how it works. You can read all the Alzheimer literature you want. But I assure you it's perfectly normal for people like her."

"Dad, you're enjoying this shit, aren't you?" Susan's eyes glinted with sudden malice.

"Of course not!" I laughed.

"No, you are! This is perfect for you. I bet you're even writing about it."

She had hit it.

"And so what if I am?" I challenged her. Something in my tone reminded me of a conversation I had with Susan when she was in college. Only the tone I was using was hers at the time.

"So what if I am?" she had said. "It's just marijuana, Dad. Like in ten or fifteen years it will all be legalized. It's only a matter of time."

Susan was twenty-three then. A full-on liberal arts major. Protesting against the Republican Party and any other authoritative force in her life. She always had a way of making me angry. I have never been what you would call a conservative myself. Rose Marie and I tried to live on equal terms. We raised our children to be free-thinkers. The world ebbed and flowed regardless of our views or marital affairs. I stayed a struggling writer,

83

often out of work as I became consumed with one masterpiece or another that ultimately got shelved and forgotten. Having children proved a great distraction. Or at least a supreme motivator for me to stay employed. Meanwhile, I crafted stories for them at bedtime, so my talents and dreams would not go completely to waste. And I loved Rose Marie because she knew I was a dreamer. In fact, she said it was the reason she loved me. And all I ever wanted was for a woman to understand me. And yet, I know there were times where she struggled to do that, much as I struggled to understand her and the disease.

Susan didn't say anything as she walked off the porch of our house. Tears still welled forth from her eyes. It probably wouldn't have helped if I said how good I thought it was for Rose Marie to berate her, or at least my mother-in-law, like that. It would only have proven how right Susan was about me enjoying it all. I admit I too was sick. Taking up writing about my wife at the lowest point in our lives seemed exploitive. But it was also proving to be profound. Any suppressed aspects of Rose Marie's mind were set free by the disease. And that she didn't turn her anger on me left me feeling secure that our love was never spoiled by my inadequacies. But Susan wouldn't understand that. If she was anything like her grandmother, she wouldn't have understood that Rose Marie loved me for my faults.

My friends often asked me at the time if it was hard losing my wife to all this. Yes, it was, but I often assured them she wasn't all that gone, yet. And having spent over fifty years with this woman, very seldom did her time jumps alarm me, for I recognized many of the faces that swam before her and morphed into the people of our past. Fifty years is a long time. Half a century. A vast reservoir of time together. And yet, like any reservoir, it threatened to dry up.

And then the final chronological jump. It exceeded my experiences with her. We were not childhood sweethearts. We met when we were both nineteen. And now she was acting like a little girl. She would call me father. And it turned my stomach. Not because I hated her own father, and not because this episode now had an air of Electra's tragedy. No. It turned my stomach because she prattled on like some lunatic. And at times she spat and drooled like a petulant infant. The words for better or worse now became most hollow. Yes. It was awful for her to distort our children with the family of her childhood. And I may have taken offense if I truly believed she thought I was her father, but the reality was I was ceasing to exist. For she called me daddy in an off way. I know she didn't really look at me and see her father. I was merely the presence of an older man to her. And if she had bothered to look at my lines and wrinkles, she would probably have called me grandpa. So it was no longer amusing. And it did hurt. It was torture. Obviously, my punishment for playing along in her delusions. For using my children as shields against her madness. For choosing to chronicle these moments for some self-fulfilling fantasy and not just for posterity. And time for us was out of joint.

And Susan was right. If I said she was wrong, then I admit it. I did enjoy it when I understood the episodes, and I found the suffering she inflicted on others rather titillating. Does this make me a monster? And as Rose Marie continued to regress, I found myself writing all the more. Any pleasure I took in her decline was only manifesting itself in my life's passion. A passion that was often denied me as I played the obedient husband, doting father, and responsible man. And Susan had me feeling guilty for using her mother so. But hadn't she used me? No. I shouldn't think that way. I freed her from her father, brother, and mother. I gave her a life. I didn't take it. But did she take mine? And did I let her or was I tricked? Mantrap? Vixen? Devil? Whore? Witch? No. This was Rose Marie. Good ole Rose Marie. Lost in time. I had to reach her. Susan couldn't understand. Susan hadn't been with her fifty years. I had. And Susan didn't want to admit that her wrinkles were, in fact, starting to make her look like her grandmother, a woman whose beauty once assured me that Rose Marie would age gracefully.

Age gracefully. Why my pathos was twinged with ridiculous humor was anyone's guess. Nothing about Rose Marie was graceful now. This irony at my youthful assumptions that the woman I had been destined to marry would age with beauty and dignity was painfully unraveling before me. This toddler stage of her disease had her stumbling and dropping things. Babbling incoherently. Pulling at my face and beard as if I were some fake Santa Claus set out for her enjoyment.

And then there was the crying. From both of us. The reservoir was being filled with tears. It needn't be dry, thought the universe. Meanwhile, nights were spent in separate rooms. Out of modesty and privacy. And avoidance of shouts of rape or murder from her end. She may still have thought of herself as Rose Marie, but who was I? I did not know.

So I waited. An inevitable Death vigil had begun. Only she wasn't in the standard coma, not really. And the nursing home graciously contained her, restrained her, force-fed her, and at times entertained her, while I helplessly just looked on. I watched a tableau of what I had often seen in movies, and on occasion encountered when I had briefly visited others who had come to the nursing home to rehabilitate, convalesce, or expire there. I could have felt guilty for not having tended to her myself, but I couldn't bring myself to being near her. But I was there. Watching. Daily. This was my torture now.

And part of me wanted to drag it out. Not see her go. And not because I was writing more or I was afraid of losing my muse. No. This was my wife. In sickness and in health. These words rang true now. And we were both sick, in the heads and in the hearts. And I watched half of me disappearing. My better half.

Then Roy came. Our oldest. Rose Marie didn't even recognize him as hers. And I longed for her to hold him in the light, like a newborn. But she hardly smiled at him. She had a classic, glazy look in her eyes now. Soulless and devoid of character. And I wanted to hit her. So hard. Snap her out of it. Bring her back to reality. Beat her into some semblance of the woman I once loved. Then Roy stayed my hand.

Holding it, unaware of the rage, or maybe somewhat cognizant of the anguish I felt, he whispered to me, "Remember that story you used to tell us kids?"

"Which one?" I chuckled, for we both knew it was a loaded question.

"The one about the good witch who sang to herself. And you said, every night children all over the world would hear her song and dream of a better place. Did that witch ever have a name?"

"No," I said, not taking my eyes off Rose Marie. "Not really. It was just one of many silly stories. "

And we stood there. My son and I. Still holding hands. For the rage I had been feeling was fading due to the gentle touch of my child's hand. And we stood. And we watched as she danced a quiet ballet for no one in particular. And she sang under her breath. And I felt calm. Something I hadn't felt in quite a long time

And then, at last, the phone call came. A death knell via our cordless phone with large buttons, which further mocked our battle with time. Somehow it still came as a shock. Coming to the rest home, I watched the orderlies attend to her final moments. I stood there amid the chaos not sure if they were trying to keep her alive or letting her go. I was immobile to intervene. Wasn't this what I had been waiting for? An end to her life? The final epilogue I needed to complete my writing? Suddenly I was appalled by all my actions. Like I was choosing to kill off my lead character to enhance the story. What heated fan mail would I receive for having done so! But she wasn't some character. This was, had been, my wife. Was my writing killing her? No. It was the disease. I was merely writing down my observations and reactions. That's what writers do. We observe. We write. We philosophize. We theologize. Sometimes detached. Sometimes not. She was detaching herself from me, this world. The writing was keeping her alive. I'm sure of it. If I went home at that instant, I was sure I could breathe life into her again. She wouldn't have to die. But this, what I was seeing, wasn't it right? Wasn't it natural? All good things and all that. But it didn't have to end. Susan might not understand, but Rose Marie, my Rose Marie, would. I could preserve her in a time loop!

All three of our children came to the funeral. And it didn't seem to matter much who said what or in what tone or what Rose Marie or I did to them. They came. And I didn't care if they came out of love for her or love for me. Or simply guilt. And I didn't care that Susan said nothing to me, but that's not entirely true. Otherwise, I wouldn't have written it all down. The fact is she was there. With Roy. With Duncan. And on the metaphysical plane: Leonard; Carol, my mother-in-law, and Thomas, the man I never wanted to be like; Harry, her lover, and all the others that had gone on before us. I can't recall crying much that day. After all, the tears in a reservoir will dry up, I'm told. Leaving us feeling empty. Who would fill me up, I did not know. But God and Susan forgive me, I knew enough to sit down and write. For writing has always filled the void that is created by guilt, or loss, or love. And now, you and I can go back to the beginning and see that love and time can both be infinite in our minds.

BLESSINGS AND PAIN
Linda Donaldson

Heart hurting for beloved godson,
Anguish for sister's wrenching reality,
Admiration for family's strong spirit,
In spite of devastation, determination prevails.

Heart yearning for a time before before
One second before the screaming flash.
I'd give my life to avoid this trial,
Sacrifice everything for a divine undoing.

Never knew such depths of despair;
Never imagined such excruciating outrage.
Breath catches, mind revolts, throat aches,
Year after year, heartfelt requests, now denied.

"Keep him safe, God, keep them all from harm"
An auntie's prayer, routine entreaty precious as breath.
Only faith and prayer can see us through this time,
This agonizing passage, this interlude.

Please, let it be an interlude in a thriving life's path,
Not an ending, not a derailment.
Only his strong example of courageous faith
In the ugly face of this debilitating hurdle keeps me standing.

Only their fortitude, their cohesion, their determination
To see this to its best possible end prevents me from crumbling,
Buffers me from the screaming self-pity of defeat.
Move a toe, move a thumb, such simple requests unfulfilled as yet.

Hang a future on the skilled caregivers,
The devoted researchers, the intrepid experimenters.
Trust the murky guesswork of medical professionals;
Choose frightening options with case-workers.

How is this our path now, so diametrically opposed
to the one we were treading before before?
Dare to hope? Pray now for a miracle. Reject despair.
Cling to faith and family and tenacious hope.

COURTING MELANCHOLIA
Joshua DeVault

She said he had a nice smile,
with eyes blue and bright,
"just keep smiling," she laughed
in her dress wrapped tight.

The smell of lilacs carried in the wind
as the stars burned holes in the night,
making up their own constellations
falling asleep in each other's arms.

Her thoughts were in his warm embrace
a troubled childhood no more
all the stress and anxiousness gone
listening to his gentle snore.

Who has been using the toothpaste the wrong way?
The toilet paper put on in reverse.
Sitting down to the ever flow of bills,
their art couldn't save them from the foreclosure curse.

He loved her more than happiness and land,
they made do—apartment to apartment,
lost vagrants stuck in a hipster world
he whispered in her ear, "we will make it through"

She said he has a nice smile,
with eyes blue and bright,
"just keep smiling," she laughed
in her dress wrapped tight.

Her art became her anger.
Nothing painted right.
Brushes hit the floor as she walked away.
He pleaded, "everything is going to be alright."

Nothing was bought because nothing was sold.
Trips to Sally's and Goodwill became date night.

But where to go when it got so cold?
He reassured himself, "everything is going to be alright."

Cashier by day, bar back by 5pm each evening.
He had no time to think, just keep working.
Minimum wage can't break even...
but all for her, he loved her, as she gave her reason:
She said he had a nice smile,
with eyes blue and bright,
"just keep smiling," she laughed
in her dress wrapped tight.

The doctor upped her medication,
she seemed to be ok. Instead of the rage,
she went into the corner to shake.
When she calmed, they got engaged.

She painted pictures of love,
he held her tight in bed,
he tried saving up for the wedding,
she wanted to be dead.

Not knowing what to do,
he gave everything to her,
she visited family and friends,
and returned in a drunken slur:

You have a nice smile,
with eyes blue and bright,
"just keep smiling," she laughed
in her dress wrapped tight.

They got married in Vegas.
Affordable, millennial quaint.
No fanfare from family, friends,
they couldn't care or relate.

She took to vodka, he drank whiskey.
He was sent home from work, told not to come back.
When the bottle was gone, he went for the meth.
She told him that she wanted her lover back.

She said he had a nice smile,

with eyes blue and bright,
"just keep smiling," she laughed
in her dress wrapped tight.

Supporting him through rehab,
He struggled. He strained.
She was addicted to his love,
sticking through the pain.

A new home. A new flat. A new life.
Instead of drugs and alcohol
they decided to get a cat.
Their life wasn't so dull.

She went off the pill,
trying each and every night.
After a year, the doctor said she couldn't.
They gave up that fight.

She said he had a nice smile,
with eyes blue and bright,
"just keep smiling," she laughed
in her dress wrapped tight.

The art sold well at the auction,
when the studio closed.
The bank took all the money.
Penniless, they went home.

The town looked charming, except
Main Street all boarded up.
But home is home,
and the bars were open all night.

They cried a little after inheriting that home.
No more family, no friends, they were alone.
She tried painting, but the arthritis was too much.
He tried working, but was always drunk.

She said he had a nice smile,
with eyes blue and bright,
"just keep smiling," she laughed
in her dress wrapped tight.

After her annual check-up,
she looked like she didn't care.
Doctor told her it was cancer,
that she would soon lose her hair

Insurance was a battle,
many things were not insured.
Financially rattled,
another bankruptcy secured.

He held her tight,
"everything is going to be alright"
while he showered in her hospital room.
No more hot water at home.

She said he had a nice smile,
with eyes blue and bright,
"just keep smiling," she laughed
in her dress wrapped tight.

She never really recovered,
though they said the cancer was gone.
She never really bothered,
whenever something went wrong.

He tried to hold her.
But she was dead inside.
She tried to talk to him.
But he had a drunk mind.

It's not like they tried to escape.
Her opioids seemed to help.
But his razor wasn't sharp enough
for him to seek out help.

She said he had a nice smile,
with eyes blue and bright,
"just keep smiling," she laughed
in her dress wrapped tight.

She created conditions to get more pills,
his condition asked where is the thrill?
They both started courting Melancholia,

cheating, both making love to sweet Mel.

Mel gave her all the medicine she wanted,
Mel gave him all the company he liked.
They both tried to hold each other tight.
But they knew something wasn't right.

Melancholia sharpened his razor,
he thought to indulge. Dreaming. Thinking.
An escape from the cycle, one last shave, time.
But he still loved her, still had feeling.

The smell of lilacs carried in the wind
as the stars burned holes in the night.
They kissed each other, as he asked,
"where have you been?"

She said he had a nice smile,
with eyes blue and bright,

"Just keep smiling," she laughed
"I love you," holding him tight.

THE HIGHWAY AND BYWAY
OF SORROW AND HAPPINESS, ROUTE 2
Joanne McIntosh

"Are we there yet?" "When will we be at Aunt Mildred and Uncle Mac's?" I kept asking. This was me when I was just a small child bugging my parents every few minutes on the very long ride from Chelmsford to Easthampton, Massachusetts.

Mom and Dad answered in unison, "Jo, stop asking, settle down and look out of the window or take a nap!"

We were off on our annual Thanksgiving journey; over the hills and through the woods to my aunt and uncle's house on Brewster Ave. in Easthampton we would go.

Back in those days, it was a very long and tedious trip down the back roads until we reached Route 2 heading toward Western Massachusetts. After all, I did not have an iPhone or iPad to keep me entertained like kids do now. Route 2 was one of the only major highways in the Commonwealth of Massachusetts at that time.

That was usually the only time that we traveled on Route 2 when I was a child. It was a long journey back then as we would travel back roads to Route 2 then all the way until we turned off Route 2 in Orange at Exit 16. Even then, we had another long hour until we arrived for our turkey dinner. There was not a Dunkin Donuts at Exit 16 as there is today, to break up the monotony of the ride. It definitely was a journey of excitement and great happiness. I loved all of the festivities and elegance of our Thanksgivings and, I sure did love my Aunt Mildred and Uncle Mac.

Route 2 has been the guardrail in many events of my life. I have traveled up and down this rural Central Massachusetts highway so many times and have lots of memories both happy and sad of those travels.

Flash forward to several years later and here I was, a college student, and Route 2 came back into my life. Mom and I set out for my college interview at Mount Wachusett Community College in Gardner. Oh, how it was snowing! We barely made it on time, but we did! Mom's knuckles were white as she gripped the steering wheel when we pulled into the parking lot. I was filled with excitement but also fear that we would slide off the road into a snow bank and I would miss my college interview.

Yea! I was accepted along with many of my Chelmsford High School classmates so my years at the "Mount" were filled with lots of fun times, very similar to high school. I moved into an apartment with a friend and lived in Gardner on Elm Street for my freshman year and several weeks of my sophomore year. It was such a happy time.

Every Friday afternoon I came home traveling down my old friend, Route 2 to go to work. My boyfriend, Bruce would drive me home as I sat there gazing at him all starry eyed. Then Sunday nights, my Mom and Dad would drive me back up my old friend, Route 2, to college after we had visited Grammy and Grandpa. Back and forth on Route 2 we would go, always happy to be traveling this long stretch of highway I knew so well. College to home and back again until…

September 23, 1968, second week of my sophomore year at the "Mount". I had a horrible feeling in the pit of my stomach when someone came into my Biology class and announced, "Joanne McIntosh, report to Dean Hogan's office!"

I rushed down the stairs, knees shaking, and as I went into the Dean's office, there was Mom and our Minister and family friend, Bill

Parsons. Mom wrapped her arms around me and choked sobbing. "Daddy died this morning."

I gathered up my belongings, packed my suitcase and off we went back down my old friend Route 2, this time the highway seemed different though, back toward home. It is now forty-nine years later and I still remember that trip, the trees passing by seemed sadder then, the highway even longer.

There is a very sharp and dangerous curve on Route 2 near the Fitchburg exit. Reverend Parsons was driving so fast, I was sure that we all would be killed right then and there. You see, my friend's Mom had been killed on this stretch of Route 2 only a few years before.

There were many more days traveling on my old friend, Route 2 as, following my Dad's passing, I decided to move home and commute to college ninety miles round trip every day; Chelmsford to Gardner and back again. Route 2 and I became best of friends.

Graduation Day came and I was accepted at Fitchburg State College! "Don't worry old friend, I am not leaving you yet." I was married and away a day or two for our honeymoon. Then a year later I had to leave my old friend, Route 2 behind temporarily as I was expecting the birth of my daughter. The day I had to take a leave of absence from Fitchburg State was a day traveling down my old friend with mixed emotions. I was sad and stressed due to leaving college but, so full of joy and happiness as I was about to become a Mommy! So many thoughts I shared with my old friend Route 2 that day!

I returned to my old friend in September back to our old routine of my traveling up and down the long stretch of highway which knew me so well.

June of the next year, I was headed back up Route 2 for graduation. Oh HAPPY DAY! I had already been teaching at Page School in Ayer for six months. My dreams were coming true.

Would you believe that after forty-six years of not traveling up and down Route 2 every day that I would say, "I am back?" Here I go; I am leaving my home town of Chelmsford and following the moving truck up Route 2. I was sobbing all of the fifty three miles to my new home of Athol, Massachusetts. I didn't want to move, but I had to move. It was a very dark and sad time in my life, but, in hindsight, I am sure my old friend Route 2 was so happy to have me back in my travels on that long stretch of highway I knew so very well.

In retrospect, it was the beginning of yet another happy Route 2 adventure. And guess what! My exit on Route 2 is the same exit that we took every Thanksgiving when I was little, Exit 16!

Now three years later, I call Athol my home. I have been up and down Route 2 riding backwards in an ambulance way too many times; I travel on my old friend Route 2 every Sunday to visit my daughter and her family and to attend church; Route 2 and I are now the best of friends. I just marvel at the beauty of the trees in the fall with their cheeks blushing with reds and wearing orange and yellow shirts. In the winter they are laden with shawls of white snow glistening in the sun. Then the sunsets are just breathtaking, saying welcome home, my friend. I guess that the journey of the rest of my life will be traveling the highways and byways of my beloved picturesque Route 2.

REMEMBERING WORLD WAR II
Phyllis Cochran

The kids in our neighborhood were not immune to turmoil. We lived in the small town of Winchendon, Massachusetts during World War II. I had started first grade in 1942 at Woodcock Elementary a year after America entered the war, and spent recess boasting about how many empty tin cans I stomped and the candy and gum tinfoil wrappings our family collected to form a ball for the war effort.

I stood with mom in a long line outside the school building waiting for a book of ration stamps to buy a five-pound bag of sugar or a pound of meat. Mom had to account for the number of people in our family before she received stamps.

We became part of an era where we could find fun in what might have been frightening for a child. When mom handed us a plastic bag of white stuff like fat with a red/orange bead in the center, we argued over which one of us kids could knead the bead into the white fat trying to release the dye in the bead and change the white fat to yellow. This chore at first seemed challenging but soon was handed off to the next child waiting a turn. After a length of time we handed mom the bag of yellow stuff. She told us it was oleomargarine, a replacement for butter to use on our toast and food.

Neighborhood blackouts became part of life. If we were romping around outside when air raids sounded; we'd race home. Mom never needed to give a second yell on those nights. We were trained to take cover. The warden on our street pounded on our front door. As a six or seven year old child, I thought the warden looked scary with his hat pulled down over his forehead. "All lights out, and curtains closed," he ordered when Dad opened the door a crack. Pulling the curtain apart, I watched this man with a flashlight in hand hike up the black street. We snuggled in bed early those nights wondering if or when a real attack might occur.

When World War II ended, the kids stopped playing. The news spread rapidly through our neighborhood. We ran over to the nearest house and listened outside one friend's window to hear the news reporter's announcement. For the first time in a long time, we sensed what freedom meant.

I remember shouting, "the war's over." The good news spread quickly. Car owners drove around honking their horns in celebration. Whistles blew. Church bells rang.

After the war, money and food were still scarce, but our parents assured us that our quality of life would improve. Finally we could go to bed at night without fear. And when sleep came, we were at peace. The "blackout wardens" returned to their normal family life.

We grew up never talking about war without retelling a few of our personal stories. What we learned from our parents during those years is fondly remembered. Today, as adults, my siblings and friends sometimes reminisce about how our fathers and mothers struggled during World War II.

Now when we face life's uncertainty, we realize how much our parent's strength and love stabilized our emotional turmoil and guided us forward. We recognize the value of what cannot be purchased with money - the love that binds a family together in tough times.

ON HEARING TRAGEDY IN THE NEWS
Steve Michaels

On hearing tragedy in the news
My heart ultimately weeps.

Then time passes.
It becomes a lost memory.

I vaguely remember praying softly that night
When the news reports it again:
There will be
A vigil
A remembrance.
Is it because the victims know
I've already forgotten?

And I realize
I created a dam
To keep their tragedy out
While I sat securely
On the other side
Of their collective, tearful memories.

What shame there is
In forgetting all the things we hear,
But I suppose
If it weren't for mental dams
We would all drown
In the reservoirs of grief.

MARIGOLD VERONA'S STRANGE ADVENTURE
Linda Donaldson

Marigold Verona tossed her long chestnut hair in the sunshine and reached her arms into the soft spring breeze. She turned to see Brett trundling the picnic cooler across the field. Youth was in their corner and the two young people were thrilled about this rare escape. Her mom had prepared fried chicken and watermelon and the ride and the scents had made them both ravenous. They had strong appetites not only for the food but for each other.

Marigold and Brett had only met a month ago when he came to do some work on the local social center's rickety roof. Their chemistry had been instantaneous and obvious to her family and friends who, naturally, had advised caution. She had never been the type to entertain romance. Marigold had always been the leader in her high school and college activities. Always sociable and always friendly, she had a wide circle of friends but never any special fellow. Her strong feelings for Brett had surprised her but he seemed as smitten as she, so her heart was contented.

May in Massachusetts is amazing when the wind keeps the mayflies at a minimum. The meadow was bouncing with wildflowers and their checkered blanket made a perfect tablecloth atop the soft grasses. As she pulled the provisions from the cooler, their eyes met and their smiles were luminous. He leaned toward her and, while caressing her check, he pressed his lips to hers. Suddenly the earth began to tremble and the trees swayed violently. A fissure opened and they tumbled into a crevasse that hadn't existed moments ago.

Deep underground, they sputtered the dirt and dust out of their mouths and blinked to adjust their eyes to the gloom. Looking around, they realized they were surrounded by a maze of tunnels. Looking up, they discovered no sky or meadow only a dirt ceiling.

"What the heck?" Brett mumbled. "Are you OK, Marigold?" He enfolded her in a bear hug and they trembled together for a few moments trying to comprehend what had happened.

"No broken bones here, what about you?" she asked and they examined each other finding minor bruises and lots of grime but no serious injuries.

"Where are we? What happened? What the heck?" they babbled simultaneously.

"Shhhh, listen." Brett instructed. "Do you hear that?" From far away down what looked like a paved tunnel they heard faint music.

Exchanging a glance, they arose and walked tentatively toward the sound. "We must be somewhere beneath Quabbin Reservoir," Marigold whispered.

Holding hands and still trembling, they walked toward some hazy light along a musty passage. Entering a huge, well-lit banquet hall, their eyes widened in wonder. A table was set with candelabra and shining silver. A chamber orchestra played on a raised dais and elegantly dressed men and women mingled around the room that was hung with rich tapestries.

"Welcome, strangers, to Nipmuck Mansion," said a gentleman wearing a powdered white wig and breeches. "I hope our invitation didn't harm you in any way. We've been waiting a century for a young couple to occupy that field so that we could expand our village and share our legacy."

Confused, Marigold and Brett stared open-mouthed at the elderly collection of elegantly dressed pioneers. Realizing that they were younger by decades than anyone present, Marigold shook her head and cleared her throat. "May I have a drink of water?" she asked.

"We have mead or cider, my dear," offered the spokesman. "Which would you prefer?" A woman dressed in wide skirts and a shawl approached with a tray of beverages in elegant stemmed goblets.

Brett chose mead and Marigold took a goblet of cider between her shaking fingers. After a sip, she managed to ask "What? Where are we? Who are you?"

"We are the early settlers of Greenwich, Massachusetts. When our graves were exhumed, we were surprised to find ourselves here surrounded in splendor but separated from civilization and unable to observe our descendants. Can you tell us what happened when the reservoir was built?"

"Your towns were flooded and your families were scattered," She told them, eliciting gasps and grumbles. "The government gave them money and most of them dispersed into the hills and valleys of western Massachusetts. Many founded or worked for manufacturing companies along the rivers but some became destitute wanderers."

"Will you join us for dinner?" asked an elegant lady who took their host's arm as they moved toward the long table. "We would like to speak with you but you must be hungry after we interrupted your picnic so abruptly." There was the hint of a twinkle in her eyes.

Brett shrugged and Marigold was too shocked to do anything but comply.

"You should know that your towns became a beautiful reservoir that provides homes for fish and wildlife, beautiful scenery for our population and water for the people of our state." She tried to assuage some of the consternation she sensed in the room. Her mind couldn't quite grasp that she was speaking to people who arrived in this area 250 years ago to build towns in a wilderness.

Brett downed the mead and looked wildly around him as they took their seats at the table set for fifty people from the 1700's. They were introduced to the first families of Enfield, Prescott and Dana as they took their seats beside the first mayor of Greenwich who had greeted them.

"Why are we here?" asked Brett when he finally found his voice. "How is this even possible? Where did you get this food, this furniture, and how are you even alive here talking to us?" His incredulity was palpable and matched Marigold's own amazement.

"We wondered that, too, for a long time," said the gentleman who had introduced himself as Major Pomeroy of Quabbin Parish. "We have aged but slowly and we have concluded that magic is the only explanation for this place."

"We are all growing tired. We believe that heaven awaits us and that we will be on our way there shortly after this long interlude," the mayor's wife explained. "We wanted somebody to know our stories first, though, and you happened to arrive at just the right moment."

As they dined on quail and pheasant with root vegetables and peaches, they all spoke lovingly of their old farms and their families. They lamented that their resting places had been so rudely disturbed and many blamed that for this unusual predicament.

"We have been happy here, though," said Marjorie after introducing herself as the Major's wife. "We often wonder about the heathens and our families and the fate of the nation we watched being born."

"Do they still tax the living daylights out of everyone who works the land?" asked Daniel Shays. "That infernal federal government was always so greedy; I hope you've put a stop to that trend."

"Well...," muttered Brett. "We try to monitor our elected officials. There are many citizens who complain but we pay our taxes so that we can fund defense and services."

Marigold chimed in. "Our country now numbers 50 states and stretches from coast to coast, you'll be proud to know." Her upbeat personality urged her to cheer up these congenial hosts even though her mind was still reeling from this abrupt break with reality. "The struggle between state's rights and the federal government continues but we are still a strong county with a bright future. You'll be glad to know that your efforts to form a commonwealth are still appreciated today."

"My name is Mrs. John Crawford," said a distinguished looking woman at the far end of the table. "I would like to know what happened to my chickens that I left in the care of my daughter-in-law." A groan went up from those assembled and many eyes rolled.

Marigold cleared her throat and shook her head. "I can't tell you that, ma'am, but I can tell you that women are now allowed to vote and to own real property!" A gasp went up around the room and many jaws dropped.

Brett spoke up, "It's been almost a hundred years since our female citizens gained the right to cast their ballots. Women are elected to serve as representatives, senators and we've even had female candidates for President!" His smile indicated that he enjoyed imparting this news that obviously amazed his audience.

"I suppose the trains now transverse the entire country," Marjorie interjected. "The Iron Horse was really taking over last I knew."

"You might not believe this, ma'am," added Marigold, "but humans have flown into outer space and even landed on the moon. We have airplanes that can take us to any country in the world!" She was warming to this role of reporter from the future.

"I'm Mrs. Ferguson," a soft-spoken woman introduced herself as the exclamations around the room started to recede. She was seated directly across the table from Marigold. "I'm glad I got to meet you. Your news is just incredible! We've all had so many questions about how life evolved."

"It's a pleasure to meet you, too, Mrs. Ferguson. I have a friend, Jolene Ferguson, who is a professor of chemistry," Marigold replied. "I believe her great-great-great grandfather was from Prescott. The family has kept pictures of the farms there as cherished heirlooms."

"Oh, I'm glad they haven't forgotten us ancestors, that's a relief!" she sighed.

The group moved to seats in front of the stage and listened to the music for an hour and then people started wandering off. Marjorie suggested that she show Brett and Marigold to separate chambers. The group dispersed and quiet descended on the strange little community. Marigold was exhausted and fell asleep soundly on a feather bed under a handmade quilt of fine linen.

Waking in the morning dew on the checkered blanket surrounded by butterflies and finches, Brett and Marigold gazed at each other and burst out laughing.

"What a dream I had!" they said simultaneously. They ate cold fried chicken for breakfast and never again spoke of their experience to each other or anyone else.

TIMES GONE BY
Joshua DeVault

Looking out the factory window,
I can see the Town Hall's clock tick by,
each hour gives a chime,
how much longer until 5?

press, press, pass,
little metal pieces in the fold,
press, press, pass,
same thing, once young—now old.

I started here when I was 14
leaving grade school behind,
by the time I was 17
my heart was blind.

The whistle blew at 3pm,
I couldn't wait to see her again.
Every Friday was ice cream at the creamery
down on old main street by the Woolworths.

She would laugh at the machine oil on my nose,
offering me her handkerchief, embarrassed my face so red,
One day I finally asked her father and later proposed.
By 18, we were married, new house, new bed.

press, press, pass,
my first child was on the way!
press, press, pass,
American Dream today!

By 25, we had 3 children,
And do they grow so fast!
The youngest suffered the polio,
into a wheel chair with the leg cast.

By 35 my 2 children could join me,
working the full 7-3.
Waiting for the whistle to blow,
home where a warm meal would be.

By 40, my oldest was drafted to war,
How busy the factory was during that time.
They only gave me three days to grieve,
When burying his body during peacetime.

press, press, pass,
the factory wasn't the same anymore
press, press, pass,
my second son joined the Marine Corp.

By 55 I was able to retire,
but I refused and kept on working,
Factory was the only life I knew,
besides my wife's warm cooking!

Still working the same machine,
as when I started at 14.
Better wage, new hours 9-5,
until the union started to rage.

Nobody seemed to agree,
production went down.
Workers started to flee
when that highway came through town.

press, press, pass,
last day of operations we were told,
press, press, pass,
same thing, once young—now old.

THE GOD OF HONEY: A LOVE STORY
Diane Kane

At eighty-nine Stuart didn't think much about the difficulties of caring for his wife Honey. Last year the doctors told him Honey had dementia. They didn't need to tell him. He knew Honey as well as he knew the palm of his own hand. He had been noticing little inaccuracies for years.

Stuart and Honey had met seventy years ago, married, built a home and raised a family. That's what people did in the nineteen forties. Stuart would say he and Honey had more than a marriage. They had something that a lot of people simply never find. They had true love.

Stuart didn't just build a home seventy years ago. He built a homestead. All he needed to do was look out his front window to behold the fruits of his labors. Over to the right past his two-story red barn sat his son's house, a sturdy log cabin constructed from the oaks grown and felled on his own property some forty years ago. Past the field of summer hay laid the winding dirt road that led to his grandson's house. In the fall he could see the smoke billowing up from the chimney. When the leaves fell from the trees, he could see the lights of the house in the chill of the night. His grandson had a fine wedding about ten years back, right in the yard where Stuart had got down on his knee and asked Honey to marry him in another lifetime.

Life hadn't always been easy. Sometimes he had wondered if it ever was. Honey had lost two children in the early years. They lay in the family cemetery on the edge of the hayfield. Many a tear had washed those little stones—side by side, heart by heart. The next pregnancy had nearly taken Honey.

The doctor said it was in God's hands. God was kind that day. He spared Honey and gave Stuart a son to carry his name.

Those were hard times, but they never went hungry. They farmed the land and raised cows and pigs, chickens for eggs and horses to lighten the workload. All earned their keep. His son grew strong and prospered on the farm. Honey was the mesh that held them all together with a smile and a prayer.

Stuart often wondered what would have become of him without Honey. He'd never admit it, but many times his faith in God had wavered. He wondered if there was a God, why good people have to suffer.

"It's not for us to question, Stuart," she would say. "Only to believe and we will be rewarded."

Sometimes Stuart wondered if the reward was worth the suffering. He would never say that to Honey. When he looked into her eyes, he knew he would suffer anything for her and never question the price. If Honey believed in God that was enough for him. He only hoped God would watch over his Honey.

Whenever the trials of life weighed heavy on Stuart's shoulders, he only needed to look to Honey for reassurance. No matter what happened, Honey's response was always, "Well, it could be worse!"

When Stuart heard the strength of belief in her voice, it was hard to disagree.

Stuart stayed with Honey all the time now. He never left her. It was true there were plenty of family nearby that would come over any time. Stuart knew it would confuse Honey and he didn't want to frighten her.

When Stuart went to the store, he brought Honey with him. He used to bring her into the store. Lately, the people and noise were too much for her to handle, so he left her in the car where she was perfectly content.

Honey had always been a knitter. She knitted Afghans for her son and his wife for Christmas and special occasions. She knitted baby blankets for the two grandchildren when they were born. She even knitted for the neighbors 'grandchildren. He couldn't remember the last time she knitted anything. Yet the knitting needles still lay beside her chair in the living room with a skein of yarn connected to them. Sometimes she would pick them up and set them in her lap. They seemed to give her comfort. Stuart started bringing them in the car with them. He would set them in her lap and say "Honey, why don't you work on this beautiful afghan while I go in the store." She would smile and pick them up. When he returned sometime later with the groceries, not a stitch was taken. Honey would still be smiling. Stuart would tell her what wonderful work she was doing.

One day it had taken a particularly long time in the grocery store. The checkout line had been long and slow. Stuart politely thanked the young clerk and hurried to the door. He didn't notice the wrinkle in the mat by the exit. He tripped and came crashing down on the floor. He got up gingerly and started to gather his scattered groceries. His leg came out from under him again. It seemed as though everyone in the store had heard the ruckus and was at his side. The manager came out of his office and insisted that Stuart allow him to call the ambulance so he could be checked out. Stuart thanked him kindly. He insisted he was fine, just a bump, and no need for a fuss. All the workers and customers had picked-up and re-bagged Stuart's groceries. They carried his groceries and helped him out to his car. He breathed a sigh of relief when he saw Honey sitting comfortably in her seat smiling at the knitting needles in her lap. He reassured all the kind people that he was just fine. The manager made him promise to call if he needed anything at all.

When Stuart got home, he gently got Honey out of the car and into her chair in the parlor. He was hobbling back to retrieve his groceries, when his son Stu happened to look out his kitchen window. Stu was an EMT, and even from that distance, he knew something was very wrong. He hurried over as his dad lifted the last bag of groceries out of the trunk.

"What happened, Dad?"

"Oh, this limp you mean? I had a little tumble at the grocery store that's all. No need for worry."

Stu was very worried. He convinced his reluctant father that he needed to go to the hospital.

Stuart had broken his hip and would need surgery.

Stu, his wife Joyce, their son Kyle and his wife Charissa all took turns staying with Honey. The day after Stuart's surgery Charissa came to pick up Honey and take her to the hospital for a visit. They talked all the way to the hospital about the fall, the hip surgery, and the recovery. Charissa was pleased with how well her gran was taking it all. Honey smiled and nodded her head.

When they pulled into the parking lot of the hospital Honey looked around.

"What are we doing here?" she demanded.

"Granny we're here to visit Granddad."

"What the heck is he doing here?"

Charissa proceeded patiently to tell Honey the whole story again as she got her out of the car and into the hospital, knowing full well that this wouldn't be the last telling of it.

They had a great visit with Stuart. He was in good spirits and so happy to see his Honey. When Charissa saw that her Gran was fading out and her Granddad looked tired, despite his attempts to hide it, she decided it was time to go.

As Charissa was helping her into her coat, Honey exclaimed, "Well it could be worse, Stuart! You could have broken your hip!"

"But gran he did--."

"You're right Honey," Stuart interrupted Charissa. "It can always be worse."

Honey smiled and kissed Stuart on the forehead.

When Stuart came home from the hospital, he noticed that Honey had regressed. He tried to ignore the signs. He knew the time was coming when she would need to have medical care that he couldn't give her. He found a good place close by where he could see her often.

Honey gradually disappeared into another world. Stuart continued to visit her every day. She rarely spoke. When she did, it was in vague and broken sentences. Still, she never seemed sad, and Stuart sat proudly by her side. He saved his tears for the ride home.

Honey was steadily fading, and the doctors had been trying to prepare Stuart for the inevitable loss. He was looking into Honey's blank eyes, wondering how it could be any worse, when he heard the voice of Honey in his head say, *it could be worse, Stuart. I could have never known you, and I can't imagine anything worse than that.*

"You're right Honey, it could be worse," Stuart said to the silent stranger in his wife's body.

He saw Honey's eyes dilate and a smile come to her sagging face.

"Stuart," she said. "It's so good to see you. I've missed you."

"I've missed you as well Honey," Stuart answered with surprise.

He saw her eyes slowly dilating back to her inner world.

"I love you," he said quickly.

Honey's lips moved in silence. He didn't need to hear; he knew what she had said.

A tear rolled down his cheek. He looked deeply into Honey's blank eyes. He was sure he saw something there. He knew it was the eternal light of true love.

He smiled through his tears and thanked the God of Honey.

ROYALSTON RHAPSODY
Sharon A. Harmon

Somewhere between any and every pristine
New England village sits our special town,
nestled like a royal nugget of gold
in a minefield of stoic rocks.

The meandering center road is spotlighted
by a white spiraled church reaching up to indigo skies,
encircled by ancient trees, daffodils
and huge, gracious houses with tales to tell.

To the south, it brags of sheep farms, a celebrated little
restaurant, where scents of good cooking hang in the air.
Railroad tracks march side by side of a river
that will take your breath away on an autumn day.

To the west, trails and mountain ridges, a scenic
overview on Jacob's Ladder, a place to view
sunsets, hawks, and a silver ribbon of river
etched into your memory forever.

Our town is sprinkled with a few schools, churches,
famous waterfalls, and endless miles
of dirt roads that interweave and meld us
into the woven fabric of each other's lives.

Beneath the quaint New England village
a well-knit community of church suppers,
fairs, town meetings, post office, and dump
gatherings, fuels camaraderie amongst Royalstonites.

Do not be deceived by this sleepy little town
in North Central Massachusetts. Amid the flora
and fauna, every curve and bend, the ever-changing skies,
you'll find a collage of writers, artists and musicians.

But, best of all, you'll find down-to-earth, caring people
from every walk of life. Those who most love it here,
lay allegiance to this peaceful little New England town.

SKY MEADOW
bg Thurston

We search all our days
for a place called home,
hoping that walls and windows
will keep us safe inside.
As our skin grows loose
over our bones and our sight
softens the landscape,
we discover home might be
hidden in a meadow
amid murmurs of green
and sun-gold blossoms rising
all around our feet. This
will be the place we return to
when we remember our lives,
knowing the shelter that held us
as the water-blue sky came down
with a peace that could hardly last.

MUTED RAINBOWS AND BUTTERFLY KISSES
Diane Kane

First light of morning dripped
sweet and syrupy like chocolate
fudge on French vanilla ice cream.
I saw the face of my aunt smiling
eyes filled with muted pastel rainbows.
She looked healthy and robust like she did
before the cancer ravaged her body,
consuming life from her lungs.
We sat and talked for what seemed
a long time. She told me she was happy,
although her lips didn't move, I believed her
because she had never lied to me before.
She gestured to the whimsy hyacinth
petals fluttering in the wind. Sprouted
lucid wings and flew, skimming my cheeks
like butterfly kisses. I wept with wonder,
turning to her empty azure chair. Breathing
musky smell of English lavender and woke
to tender comfort of the sparrow's song.

TIME'S RESERVOIR
James Thibeault

Memories of the past have drained away. A cork at the bottom of a lake has been pulled. Drip by drip, it has emptied until dry—cracked earth above. This is how I feel when I am sitting alone on a couch, Friday night, surrounded by my friends. Chatter, screams, and laughter fill the room while I press hard into the sofa, trying to feel its soft comforts. I nurse the remains of my eighth beer and try to remember all the good times I had with these people. Weren't these my best friends? Didn't I laugh and cry with them before? It was hard to tell, college was so long ago. Most of the memories were gone. Only small puddles of the past lay dormant in the mud.

We were inseparable, spending late nights at diners and weekends in bars. The endless parties made us the talk of the campus. I treated all of these guys like my brothers. Then, the future happened. My so-called brothers graduated, started their careers—their families—and left me in the past. I clung to the good times, but the past has a way of evaporating its content. What used to be a sea of pleasant memories is now just a few scattered drops of 'Hey, remember the time…' or 'Wasn't it great when…'

Why didn't I just make new memories with these guys? Here we were, together, and we could create some incredible moments that we could talk about for ages. Unfortunately, the future has created a barrier between me and the others. All of them no longer want to talk about girls, video games, life, and love. Instead, they have to talk about their 401k and what is the best way to get on RT 495 South in order to avoid traffic. All of it is so boring.

"So I said to my manager," says Jake, the leader of the pack, "'Those files aren't going to sort themselves.' And he says back to me, 'Well, you better call technical assistance and request a 54b, otherwise you're going to have to file a transcript protocol that is gonna leave you nowhere.' Can you believe he had the nerve to tell me that?"

The other members of the old fraternity laugh, but I have no clue what he said. All of them went into business after college while I decided to teach middle school Social Studies. The rest of the guys were so successful, they were driving the latest cars and talking about their vacation homes at the Cape. Here I am the poor and uninteresting loser who has to listen to their success stories. It is almost too painful to bear.

"Tyler," says Jake, nudging my arm. "Are you alright?" He and the others laugh. "You better lay off the drinks. It looks like the couch is about to swallow you whole."

"I'm fine," I say and procure a cheap smile. That seems to pay the toll and the others go back to laughing. I down the rest of the beer, and then walk to the kitchen. My path is not straight but angled to the left. Still, my weary legs push to the right. Jake's legs rest on a coffee table. Before I have a chance to say 'excuse me,' my legs do not get the info to stop. I tumble and fall to the ground like a failed gymnast.

"Okay, buddy," says Jake. "Time to get you some fresh air."

The others laugh while Jake pulls me up from under my armpits. I am surprised how easily he was able to set me on my feet. In college, he was often mistaken for five Popsicle sticks. Since then, his muscles rip his shirts frequently. One of his massive arms steers me to the kitchen and toward the front porch.

"Hold on," I say. "Let me get another drink first."

"Let's get a breather, and then we'll see."

I didn't want to argue, so I let him guide me outside. The harsh November wind hits me in the face. Instantly, my eyes widen and my jaw shivers. It is too cloudy to see the stars, but that doesn't stop Jake and me from sitting on the stoop and looking up. Occasionally, a car drives by and lights some trees with its high beams. Other than that, the wind is the only thing that moves and makes a sound.

"Thanks for inviting me," I say.

"Why wouldn't I invite you?"

"I don't know, we haven't talked in like a year."

"So? Best friends can set the train right on track no matter how long it's been."

"Yeah," I say sighing. "But best friends actually see each other too."

"Jesus, I'm trying to cheer you up, but you've been a pain in the ass all night."

"Sorry."

"Are you sure you're alright?"

"Just drop it! I'm fine!" I shouted, a bit taken aback at my own response.

"Oh," he says. We listen to the wind. Jake and I used to spend late nights studying for our philosophy final, but mostly it involved us getting drunk and discussing life and our future. Jake wanted to be a writer, full time, and change the world with radical narratives and views on life. He believed people could change if they read the right words. I changed when I listened to him talk. Jake used to write poems that would have me staring up at the sky, saying 'damn.' Now, he never writes. Instead, he drafts thousands of emails to the shareholders and makes sure communication is "top notch" throughout the company. Fascinating stuff, he tells me. However, it never makes me go, 'damn.' Yet, he's says he's happy—so I should be happy for him, right?

Jake slaps me on the back. "Hey, I need to check on Isabel to see if she crawled out of her crib. Whenever there's company, she tries to sneak out. I swear she's like a raccoon—wide awake at night. I talked to the doctors, and they said it's just a phase. I don't care if it's a phase because that kid is so cranky during the day. Half the time, she just falls asleep when Monica tries to feed her. We read somewhere that popping into her room at night gives her security that we never left. Maybe she thinks we're abandoning her. How's that for some Freudian shit?"

"I thought you were going to check up on her. Why are you still talking?"

"You know what?" barks Jake, rising to his feet. "I'm really trying here. I don't know what's gotten into you, but sober up, put on a smile, and come back in when you're ready. I didn't invite you here just so you can make a fool of yourself."

"Whatever."

He is about to say something else, but after tensing his fists a couple of times, he groans and goes back inside. I let the cold numb my fingers and lips. Was he really my friend? I try to remember all the fun times we had years ago, but only fragments come to mind. Our senior year, we had decided to throw a competition to see who could drink the most vodka and peanut butter at the same time. Peanut butter was placed on a saltine cracker and had to be chased by a shot of the cheapest vodka. Whoever survived the longest was the winner. It was hard to call me a champion because I usually ended up puking. The rest of those nights had dripped away. Only bits of time splashed around in my head.

I stay on the porch for God knows how long. When Jake returns, he isn't too happy to see me still there.

"Holy shit! You must be a popsicle right about now!"

I replied with a smirk, "You remember when I used to call you a set of five popsicles?"

Jake lets out a solid laugh. His wide chest lifts and looks up at the sky. "Yeah, I remember. It's hard to imagine that I used to be so skinny. But hey, when you start doing protein shakes, it's hard to keep these muscles down. They just start exploding. Did I ever tell you the time when I benched 270? I wasn't even planning on it, I was slightly hung-over from the night before, but I was cranking out 240 no problem. So I said 'What the hell' and went for it."

"Wow," I say, choosing that moment to throw in a laugh as well.

"Oh forget it. You don't understand. 270's a big number."

"So is 1,000."

"Yeah, but can you even bench … Whatever."

We continued looking out into the black.

"I wish…" I said slowly. "We had more in common."

"We have plenty in common."

"Jake, I couldn't care less about your kid or your muscles."

"Goddamnit, you know I'm really trying here. But you're not making this easy, Tyler. Hell, the other guys didn't even want to invite you. But I said, 'No, guys, he'll be fine. Just don't bring up his job.' Instead, I get this whiny little turd who won't stop feeling bad about himself. I don't care how much money you make, how many papers you have to grade. You seem to be the only one who is embarrassed about your choices. Do I have regrets? Of course I do, but you don't seem me moping about it like you. It's time to move on."

"Well now I want to stick around."

"Come on," Jake says, defeated. "I'll drive you home."

"I'm fine."

"Oh yeah?"

"I guess you haven't worked the muscles in your brain because I said 'I'm fine'."

"Get the hell out of my house!"

"I'm already out of your house."

"Then get off my property."

"Fine."

"Good."

Jake slams the front door. I stand up, feel the blood rush to my head, and then drop back down. After a few seconds, I stand back up and my legs hold. In the dark, I press the unlock button repeatedly until my car's headlights keep flashing like a strobe light. When I reach the driver side, I hear the front door open.

"Tyler," says Jake. "Come back inside. I'm sorry."

"No," I shout back, "We're done. I'm done with you, the fraternity, and the good times we had."

"You're still drunk."

"Whatever."

"No, not whatever. Get your ass back inside."

"Screw you."

I open my car door and step inside. When I turn on the ignition, I make a good effort to rev the engine while it's in park. Everyone from inside the house looks out the window. Jake walks up to the car and taps on the driver-side window. I roll it down just enough so he could hear me.

"I'm not going back in," I say.

"You're a stubborn son-of-a-bitch. You know that?" Jake says back.

"Goodnight. And tell the other guys that I wasn't feeling well."

"I think they got the message."

"So…we'll meet up soon?" I say half-heartedly.

"Yeah, Tyler, we'll meet up soon," Jake says, looking away from me. He taps the top of the car and walks back into the house. When he closes the front door, I drive away and park around the corner. After a few minutes of crying, I pass out with my head on the steering wheel.

The rest of that night drained away as well.

DOORWAYS
Sally Sennott

In mythology Janus is the Roman god of beginnings, gates, transitions, time, doorways and passages.

Janus had double booked a barber appointment.
He stood me up for a haircut.
Janus is the god of time.
The new lunch date showed promise.
"I was up and fully dressed," Janus said,
"With face washed and beard trimmed."
But Janus has a secret he doesn't share.
"I think I'll lie down for just a second,"
"Take me down the passageway …"
Janus is the god of doorways.
He says he couldn't hear the doorbell,
Or the persistent knocks on the door.
He didn't hear the cell phone ringing
Three times in quick succession.
Deep in a heroin nod, Janus dreamed on.
Nirvana is his preferred reality.
He simply spaced out again.
Janus looks forward and back.
"So very sorry I missed our luncheon date," he says.
"Are you okay?" I loyally ask.
"Don't leave me," Janus pleads.
Should I walk away?
Will I catch my breath?
I will not go through his revolving door.
It's time to turn and walk away.

A BOTTLE OF TIME
Diane Kane

In 1973 my favorite song was Jim Croce's "Time in a Bottle." My bottle of choice that year was Boone's Farm Apple Wine. Jim Croce poetically filled his bottle with memories. I, on the other hand, would drain my bottles and fill them with memories I'd rather forget.

The drinking age was eighteen. I had just turned sixteen. This didn't deter me in my pursuit of alcohol. I saved my lunch money all week. Although I'd been known to hide my emotions in a big slice of chocolate cake with buttercream frosting, cafeteria food was not something I wasted money on.

Friday nights I counted my change and headed for the corner of Pleasant and Main Street. All the boys with cars and brains in their pants would cruise the "strip" in hopes of scoring. Most were old enough to purchase alcohol, or they had fake ID's. I put out enough to be worth the trip to the packy. First, second base tops, so far I hadn't exchanged my virginity for the purchase of a cheap bottle of booze. I can't say for sure I wouldn't have come to that had it not been for the timely breaking of a bottle.

I grew up in rural western Massachusetts. Maybe "grew up" isn't the best way to describe my journey. I aged in some ways too quickly, but my morals didn't always add up. It wasn't a big surprise. The apple didn't fall far from the tree, as the saying goes. Alcohol was literally in my blood. My mother was so intoxicated when she gave birth that they had to detox me.

I didn't have any choices when I was born, but I do now, at least that's what my therapist told me. Easy for him to say, sitting in his leather chair with pencil and paper in his nicotine-stained hands, judging me.

"Debbie, you are better than that bottle," he said.

"The last time I heard that I was in the front seat of a '69 Dodge Dart, offering my body to Andrew Dalton," I laughed. "The idiot refused me."

I had turned seventeen, and Boone's Farm wasn't providing me with the buzz I desired. I stepped up my game to Tango, a cheap mix of vodka and orange flavor. It did the trick for a while, but the next step came quicker. By that time I had a job at McDonald's. I worked weekends in my brown and white uniform, taking orders with a smile. My happiness didn't come from waiting on insolent kids and clueless parents. I was reveling in anticipation of getting out of work before the package store closed. Now that I had real money, it was top shelf for me. I actually thought myself something of a connoisseur of alcohol. Whiskey was now my choice of poison. Five Star, to be exact.

I'd take a big swig right out of the bottle. Glasses were for pussies. The slow burn down my throat, through my chest into my gut, made me feel alive and slightly immortal. Nothing could hurt me. My magic shield was a bottle of alcohol.

The night Andrew stopped to check on me, I was just about to polish off a pint. I was looking for a sucker to go to the package store and buy me another. Andrew was not one of the cool guys, but he was eighteen and had a car. He pulled to the side of the road and rolled down his passenger window.

"Are you all right, Debbie?" he asked.

"Just peachy, Andrew. You want a taste?" I stumbled over to his car. "It's Andrew, right?"

I knew very well who he was. He was a year ahead of me in school. I would watch him hold the door for girls who couldn't give him the time of day. He always said "Yes Ma'am" and went out his way to help girls with their books. I wanted some boy to treat me like that. I wished he was my boyfriend. *That's just stupid talk, what would I want with him I asked myself.* But sometimes I couldn't stop thinking about him.

"Why don't you get in my car and I'll give you a ride home?"

He jumped out and opened the door for me. I slid along the bench seat to the middle. When he came around to the driver's seat, he looked surprised to have me right next to him.

"I don't want to go home." The fierce burn of Five Star had melted into a warm numbness. "Why don't you drive by the packy and pick me up another pint?"

I could just use him and ditch him I thought. At least that's what my tough whiskey drinking ego said. The sad little girl deep inside me said, *I wish I could make him mine.*

Screw that sad little girl. She never gets what she wants.

"You don't need another pint," Andrew said.

"Don't tell me what I need." My voice snapped, and he jumped back. I hate when I do that.

Jim Croce's soothing voice came on the radio. "Time in a Bottle, my favorite song," I said. "Can you turn it up?"

"It's my favorite song too."

I started singing, and he joined in. For two minutes and twenty-nine seconds, time stood still. I didn't need a bottle or anything else to make me happy. When we sang the last line, about finding the one we had been looking for and I believed it. The look in his eyes said he believed it as well.

I started kissing his mouth furiously. He pulled the car to the side of the road. His heart was beating hard against mine. He ravished me with desire, and I longed for more. When he stopped short at my waistline, I unbuttoned my jeans and guided his hand. He fought back. I massaged his crotch, and he pushed my hand away. The spell was breaking.

"What the hell is wrong with you?" I asked.

"I don't want to do it like this."

"Like what?" I said. "You're turning me down? What are you some kind of idiot?" I tried to give him the gift of my virginity, and he didn't want it. My eyes burned with the sting of rejection.

"I usually don't lower myself to rednecks like you. It was just going to be a pity screw anyway." I pushed over against the passage door. "Take me to the package store. This bottle is empty."

He pried the bottle from my hand and threw it out my window. It shattered on the sidewalk. I stared in disbelief at the broken pieces of my obsession.

"Why did you do that?"

"Don't you get it, Debbie? You're better than that bottle of shit. You're something special."

"Just not special to you." My tough drunk ego spit out the words while my soft insides longed to hear him tell me more.

"I've liked you since 7th grade. I know you probably don't even remember me then. I wasn't good enough for you, and I'm still not." He looked at me with his soft brown eyes. "You're beautiful and smart, and when you're not drinking, you're sweet and funny." I hung on his words. "I've seen you at school with the handicap kids. They love you, Debbie."

"Stop watching me," I shouted and leaped from the car. Sobs wrenched my body as I ran to a house I was familiar with. I walked in the basement door where a group of kids always hung out. Smoke and music poured from the room. I must have looked terrible, my nose running, mascara down my cheeks, sucking in the sobs that wouldn't stop. I could see the disgust in their eyes.

"Have a little too much to drink?" one girl asked.

"Again?" another finished. They all laughed.

"I'm out of here," said another, as they all headed for the door.

I looked around and had the feeling I'd ended up in a pigsty. I'd always considered myself slightly better than these swine. Yet, here they were turning up their collective noses at me and leaving the pig pen.

It seems that alcohol had aided me in deceiving myself. When faced with this reality, I took a look in the mirror and was surprised at what I found.

I signed myself into a clinic. It wasn't easy. The DT's, the headaches, the burning need in my gut. Somehow I made it through all that, but it wasn't the end.

"You've quit drinking, but that's just the first step," my therapist said. I wanted to step on him.

I managed to pull together the tattered pieces of my life. I graduated from college and got a job working with the mentally disabled. I made a decent life for myself. Myself being the key word. I dated now and then but found the guys to be either too overbearing or too needy. I couldn't deal with the drama.

It seems that it wasn't the alcohol that molded my personality. My personality molded me into an alcoholic. Now that I didn't drink, I replaced my addiction with something else. My something else was excessive self-indulgence mixed with a big cup of self-pity. Perhaps physically healthier, but just as mentally debilitating.

At Christmas, I decided to go to the mall and buy myself a diamond necklace. After all, no one else was going to buy it for me.

Walking down the central aisle of the mall, swinging a cute little pink bag with a white handle, I felt the burn of satisfaction in my gut. I had scored a fancy black hinged box with a striking two-karat diamond necklace cradled inside. I was high on the thrill.

My eyes turned toward the sound of boots, clicking on the shiny tile floor. A nice looking guy was walking toward me with confidence in his step. His tan flannel shirt fit snug across his muscular chest, tucked in at the waist of western cut jeans. In my imagination, he tipped his hat and said, 'Howdy ma'am.'

In actuality, he was saying, "Hi Debbie."

Startled back to reality I realized it was Andrew Dalton standing in front of me waiting for a reply.

"Andrew," I stuttered. "What a surprise."

"You look great," we said at the same time and laughed. It felt nice.

"It's good to see you," he said.

"You too."

"I'm here with my wife," he said quicker than he had to. I hoped he didn't see me flinch.

"Oh, married huh? Well, I'm not surprised. Kids?"

"Two, a boy and a girl."

"It sounds just perfect. "

"Yes," He wiped the palms of his hands on his jeans. "Maybe we could double-date sometime, go out for drinks?"

I smirked. Andrew was always the diplomat.

"I'm not with anyone… and I don't drink anymore." He got the answers to the questions he wanted to ask, but he still didn't look satisfied.

"That's good. Well, not the part about not being with anyone."

"Guess I'm still looking for the perfect guy." He was standing right in front of me, and now I couldn't have him. He must have seen the melancholy in my eyes.

"Debbie," he reached his hand out. "I wish I…"

"Oh please don't." The slap in my words made him step back. *Why do I always do that?*

I smiled, trying to keep him from turning away. "Hey, remember this?" I sang the familiar sentiments of Jim Croce. My voice was low and warm.

His eyes sparkled. He started to sing with me but his voiced faded off.

Andrew took a deep breath and let it out slowly between his lips. I wanted to reach my hand up and touch his face.

"Well, I've got to go," he said. "My wife, she will be wondering."

"I need to get going too." The moment was gone. "Take care, Andrew."

"You too." He turned and walked away. I stood and watched him cut a path through the crowd. Just before he turned the corner, he stopped and looked back. I waved. He tipped his hat and smiled. It was what I had waited for.

I heard Jim Croce telling me, "But there never seems to be enough time to do the things you want to do once you find them."

I dug the fancy black hinged box out of the pink bag with the white handle, opened it and removed the diamond necklace. I held my obsession tight in my hand and resented the power it held over me.

The expensive trinket sounded like small change when it hit the bottom of the red Salvation Army kettle.

"Bless you," said the volunteer.

"Thank you," I said

Time to move on.

SANDS OF TIME
Kathy Chencharik

There was a time, not long ago
When people went to work
And they had a sense of purpose
Whether carpenter or clerk.

Their workplace was secure
They knew someday they'd retire
And spend their golden years
Rocking slowly by the fire.

Somehow, things have changed
Nothing's sacred anymore
One day you may be working
And the next, locked out the door.

Big business doesn't care about
Your name that's on a page
They'd rather move their company
And pay the minimum wage.

Why should they care about your fate
When they can walk away
Lining their own pockets
With the savings from your pay.

If you've worked for fifteen years
For twenty, or twenty-four
And you think you've got it made
Think again, not anymore.

A secure job is in the past
No matter how far you climb
It's like a well-worn photograph
Faded by the sands of time.

THE MAKING OF HEADLINES IN 1964
Steve Michaels

The King still lives
While Beatles are For Sale.
Jack was shot in November
His Camelot nearly crumbles,
But the other stays
Strong on Broadway.
Coretta loves her Martin
Who is now motivated
More than ever.
At the boxoffice
Former My Fair Lady
With "Just a Spoonful of Sugar"
Wins the hearts
Of Dr. Strangelove.
CBS orders up pilot
For boldly going
While NASA is working on
Saturn and Gemini.
Davie Jones is transformed
Soon to become a Bowie
To Explore Other
Space Oddities.
Walt wins Freedom's Medal
All while Nelson loses his.
Cassius becomes Mohamed
To prophesy the Downfall
Of Foreman and Fraizer.
A Fiddler plays his way
Down Broadway
While a movie house delights to
The Sound of Music.
In other news:
The Fight for Civil Rights
Is anything but Civil:
Malcolm is
About to perish

At the hands of
Black Zealots
Whose own Hatred
For White Supremacy
Defies his own.
This will occur
only months after
They announce
The World's Fair.

And now for My Two Cents:
If seven souls
For each deadly sin,
Be washed ashore
On Gilligan's Island,
Then Mr. John Dunn is incorrect.
But if those souls
Should symbolize us all:
Then Every Man is an Island
And that's just the way it is.

Thank you
And Goodnight.

TEN DAYS AT THE SPANDAU PRISON
Dennis F. King

I woke up one day and decided it was time to man up and do something good with my life, so I joined the U.S. Army. I knew a war was raging in Vietnam, but other guys my age were over there serving our country. The fear of dying faces us as we get closer to danger. I was not thinking of the bad things but thought of seeing the world and doing my duty to the country I live in.

My luck was with me because I was sent to the Berlin Wall in Germany, then a "hot spot" in the Cold War. The world is always a place of battles here today, gone somewhere else tomorrow, it seems. We were considered to be city soldiers being stationed there. Our training concentrated on taking possession of city building and fighting an aggressor at that time, the Soviet Army.

One day we all were ordered to "fall out" for a morning formation where a roll call is made. Each unit leader reports those present for duty and any on "sick call." The true unit strength is determined that way, every day. Today there seemed to be some private talks going on with the platoon leaders, all leaning into the huddle and then an announcement was made.

There is a saying in the Army to "never volunteer for anything" It is a warning, but I am not very smart at times and like a gamble. I had joined the army, unlike most soldiers who were drafted into the service reluctantly. We all served together but guys like me, a volunteer, were told never to complain because "You asked for it."

The top non commissioned officer spoke to us in a serious tone.

"I need eighteen volunteers for a special assignment, step forward if willing to help me out." I moved right up to the front and was directed to join the newly formed group to the side. He called out the names of three sergeants, at random to join us.

He then announced that we were going away for ten days and ten nights on a very important mission. "There will be plenty of marching and close sleeping quarters, no other duty but to be there and only there."

The best part was that when we returned after this trip, there would be three days leave given to each of us if we did not "screw up" as a unit and each individual. We were all happy and let out a yell, but then he gave us the bad news. He said that we would be confined to one building, day and night, unless on guard duty and there would be no drinking of alcohol permitted either. Then he said, "And no chasing hairy legged frauleins around at night."

The rest of our company laughed at us now knowing we were looking at a weird trip ahead but it was something different to do, I like change. The top officer stepped forward to speak to his company, and we were ordered "at ease," which means to relax in place and now listen without interruption. We all listened carefully to his words because leaders speak once and do not repeat themselves.

Then he turned towards us in this group of troops and spoke directly to us in a lower than normal voice. "You will be serving at the Spandau Prison where inside the walls is the last Nazi prisoner, named Rudolf Hess, Hitler's sidekick from the start of the Nazi's. You all know we conquered them and he is now the last man being held there. You will stay there, march as if you were in a parade in front of me."

Our next officer continued the briefing by saying, "Prisoner #7 is not allowed to be spoken to, no televisions or radio for him, all part of his punishment of isolation." The conversation ended with him saying that we were now going to be part of history. "You will guard a World War II prisoner, during two other wars going on elsewhere." Lastly, he said, "Serve us well, stay awake and remember your orders are, shoot to kill if anyone approaches the prison walls."

My new group was ordered to gather up our few toiletries, clean underwear and we would be wearing our summer uniforms, tan khakis. I was allowed one book to read; I took my copy of *Great Western Philosophers* by Bertrand Russell, looks like I will have plenty of book time and nothing else. Our trucks will be leaving in an hour, so we all hustled to be ready. At the appointed hour we climbed into our two and a half ton trucks, drove across the city to the British Sector, in the Spandau district.

We have arrived at the prison, ready for the unknown and this man behind the walls of brick. The man inside the uniform becomes different in many ways once you put it on. The feeling of power is conveyed with the weight of medals, insignias and other accoutrements. There is a pride being allowed to wear it and to represent those that provided it for the willing. You are the thoughts, hopes and the protector of your side in the battles of war. When you take it off and hang it up, there is a transformation that takes place. Now the person is naked to the world until you put on other garments. Your impression of others will be totally different now and the playing field becomes equal. I have worn both outfits and know this first hand.

I felt that way every day as I dressed for duty in the Army to face the world. The public citizens just watched us pass by, looking at our faces, as our vehicles rumbled down their cobblestone streets. We all sit erect, rifles standing in front of us, a show of force, looking like dogs with a low "growl" in our appearance

Our trucks stopped in front of an old red brick barracks, we moved in, carrying our duffel bags and rifles. The one big room has high ceilings and tall windows like a chapel, but it never was one. The room was divided into four areas with six bunk beds in three sections. A long table with chairs as a quiet reading and writing area occupies the fourth section. There is a room with a door to our right with a kitchen, eating tables, a radio but no television. There are a chessboard, playing cards, and a Foosball table but a large sign on the wall says "quiet." This place was our home for ten days in mid-August and like everything else here, unreal. We are broken up into three guard duty groups of six - squad A, squad B, and squad C. Each group slept in their own areas for a reason because when one squad was on duty, another group was going to bed.

It was a grueling schedule of three hours marching in a guard tower and then six hours off duty. We had to learn to be sensitive to others as our sleep cycles all differed. Our off time was spent taking a nap and then eating, polishing our boots, cleaning our weapons and getting ready for the next tour.

We all knew each other as part of a bigger unit of a hundred soldiers in a frontline infantry company. Here we were clustered into something different, in a building we could not leave except to march out for duty again. Each six-man squad formed into two columns of three each with a sergeant of the guard joining us.

The routine was to proceed to the front gates of the prison silently and then halt. The doors opened with a loud squeak as we were ordered to "forward march" down a hall. Next, the group went out the open back door into the courtyard and then a left turn called out in a low voice "column left." The trained soldier knows to count in his head, one, two, then follow the command, whatever it is. Timing is everything when marching and in music plus practice does make perfect.

The path below our feet was beaten deeply into the ground as unnamed feet had marched here before us. Each time we stopped at one of the six guard towers, a soldier would leave us to replace the guard there ending his stint, now joining us. We proceeded to walk on the beaten path to each guard tower, quickly changing the guard, one joins our formation, and the other soldier hurries upstairs to his post. A quick glance down to the group acknowledges it is time to march again.

When the group left the front gate, it was now all team A guards replaced by my B team being up in their towers. Like most people, they were tired and wanted to go eat, shower and go to bed. Everyone felt the strain it had on us, but we had done harder than this before, so we only mumbled under our breaths.

I recall one morning just after three A.M. we seven marched back from the prison and halted at the front door of our quarters. It was raining hard as we unloaded our rifles and cleared them, then quietly entering the building. The lights were all out as we all entered the Mess Hall area with a door behind us and the lights on brightly in here.

A soldier always tends to his weapon daily, especially after it is rained on, clean it now or rust tomorrow. We all took off our wet boots and socks, threw our wet uniforms into a special hamper of dirty laundry. Each day food, laundry, and the mail were delivered to us, the same food the guys back at the base were eating.

This night had been hot, being mid-August, windy and constant rain blowing sideways at times. While up in our powers we marched with our rifles resting on our shoulders like tin men. Around and around the ten-foot sides we marched thru the night, occasionally stopping.

A soldier stands at attention, erect, heels together and feet slightly parted with hands flat by your side. When you have a rifle, it rests on your right shoulder with the butt or bottom of it in the palm of your right hand.

The right forearm is extended forward with your elbow tucked in against your side, this is called "shouldered arms." If commanded to "parade rest," the soldier only spreads the legs apart to allow a strong stance, repositions the rifle on the ground, butt against his toe. The hand holds the barrel with the right arm extended.

The most important moves are done during the marching process where the legs and the arms move together or separately. We are told to "forward" march, and immediately we step off, right leg first in unison. Often we were ordered to "present arms," which is repositioning our weapons in front of our body, straight up and down, an armed salute. If we were marching a long distance the command to "right shoulder arms" might be changed to "left shoulder arms." This allowed us to switch which side we carried the weapon on to get some blood flowing. Sometimes if we marched past a four-star general, we would be ordered "eyes right," moments before we passed by. The soldier on the right side kept his eyes forward ensuring we stayed in a straight line.

When we were up in our watchtower, it was strictly forward march and parade rest for three hours, nonstop. There was silence inside the walls and outside too in the middle of the night. The rain and my own sweat made me feel soaked and wondering what we were doing here.

While we cleaned our weapons, oiled them and checked their action, it occurred to me to ask them, "Did anyone get wet?" Everyone sat up straight, gave me a dirty look and scowls while shaking their heads. No one dared to make noise at that hour, but it reminded us that we all got wet, felt very alone and wished for a bed, back home.

The next morning we were awoken by the smell of breakfast and our growling stomachs. The trick in the service is to get in line early to get the best food, it is hotter and plenty there but if you wait too long, you get the last of it. I liked the hot coffee best being from New England, but my buddy from Florida wanted a Coca-Cola to wash down his bacon and scrambled eggs.

The toast was always hours old, cold and stiff, never hot and oozing in real butter, the way I yearned for it. Later in the day when the chipped beef in white sauce was delivered for dinner that toast softened up a little, served as S.O.S., "shit on a shingle." I learned to like it as a meal that would fill my belly until the next morning when eaten at seven at night. Desserts were always plain white cake, pudding, and Jello. The favorite of everyone was "hot dogs and beans" night with potato chips on the side.

There was a day when one of the other guys from team A was eating with us, and he mentioned that he had seen the "old man" walking around out back in the gardens. He commented that the guy looked like any old man wandering around "looking lost." We all laughed but had no knowledge of him other than he was prisoner number seven.

The system of us rotating shifts every six hours for my team and then to different towers each time continued at all hours of the day or night. He was allowed out once a day for one hour, weather permitting after lunch from one o'clock on to exercise. I had studied the back area there one evening while on duty with old gardens now overgrown here and there but neglected. This meant that one guard a day would be back there, in the rear tower to see him if at all.

My chance had never happened to be at that hour, and finally one day we were about to go on duty for the noontime to three P.M. shift. I asked a fellow team member if I could swap posts with him so I could see the prisoner, maybe. He said "Sure, I would just as soon shoot him, means nothing to me."

That summed up the attitudes of all of us because this whole experience was annoying to us and was no fun at all. It was all business, perfect pressed Khaki uniforms, highly polished boots, marching for nine hours a day. We were used to some freedoms from duty, but here, it was stay inside or go march.

That afternoon I marched in my tower for an hour when I heard a door close and then saw a short man move quickly around the other beaten in the ground path. He walked along the narrow path for one while glancing side to side, looking for unauthorized objects and then disappeared from view.

I continued to march as perfectly as I could because peering eyes were always watching us. Our leaders had briefed us that our duty here should reflect how highly trained and disciplined we are. We were ordered to shoot intruders too close to the outer wall and not speak to the man, inside this place.

There was a motion I caught out of the corner of my eye as I turned a corner on my right side. I came to "parade rest" as required in stopping. I then stood still and looked straight ahead, but my eyes looked down and around slowly. I was excited that I might see the prisoner today when suddenly he appeared. The path was beaten into the grass by him, walking around the small area back there in the shape of a horse racing track.

Suddenly he appeared in my view. I studied his posture first, hunched over with his arms behind his back and hands together. The gait was that of a tall person with long legs but moving slowly as if counting the steps. The hair on his head was thinning, combed straight back and he looked to me to need a shave, his frame thin. Maybe he felt me looking at him, or it was a habit to look up at the tower where a soldier walked, every minute of every day.

I saw him look up at me, then look back down when suddenly he stopped and gazed up at me. There was no expression on his face or mine as my first thought was that he seemed shocked to see someone. We continued to look into each other's eyes for a long moment like two strangers about to acknowledge each other, both of us human beings.

It seemed like I was caught in a moment of importance being here and looking at him, but then my mind raced to the book at the front gate guard post. The book told of him, long ago a famous military man, a leader of those considered the most evil men in recent centuries. If I had not read that book and learned about his past of hate, mayhem, and death in his uniform, my thoughts would have been different.

The moment came when I broke my attention from him, came to attention and then shouldered my rifle and went back to marching my post. I was shaken inside knowing I had looked at him so closely, felt guilty turning away from an old man being ignored down there but also knew he deserved this punishment, this infamy for the rest of time. I continued my shift, and later that day I told my team members about that moment. They all agreed that it was better I saw him than any of them.

The prisoner lived out his life sentence, alone for twenty-five years within those walls at Spandau Prison until he used a rope to hang himself at ninety-two years old. He chose to be part of the most brutal army in our recent history. Without his uniform covered in eagles and swastikas, he was just an old man.

THE BULLY OF 33RD STREET
Joshua DeVault

I can't cry

It started as a simple look,
curt, menacing,
he hurled it.

It bounced off my chest,
I watched it fall into
a muddied reservoir forming by my feet.

I took a step forward:
   don't make eye contact
      walk faster, cover the face,
         don't look back.
I looked back.
I didn't listen.

He laughed with his friends,
proving himself in front of them,
he aimed at me, and shot these words:

   "Keep on walking you fucking faggot!"

This time it didn't bounce off.
It pierced me.
    Bleeding.
     Little red reservoir forming by my feet.

Don't make eye contact,
walk faster,
cover the face,
don't look back.

I went home
a reservoir of emotions flooding by my feet.

I cried.

DECIDING TO LIVE IN 1983
Linda Donaldson

By the time I got to Flagstaff, it was late afternoon. After a long day of driving west, I headed north and found a spot on the very edge of the Grand Canyon as the sun was setting. There I sat with my legs dangling and looked straight down for about two miles. Spectacular, awesome, breathtaking; these words can't even begin to express the glory of that space. From my perch on the edge of the precipice, the mighty Colorado River appeared as a tiny sparkling thread running through vast canyon walls striped with golden colors interspersed with darker layers. Trees and boulders along the river's edge looked like toys from that vantage point.

It occurred to me that if I just leaned forward a bit, I could lose my balance and take one last glorious breath as I hurled myself over the crest. I remember thinking that I could avoid all the headaches of a divorce, that I could avoid having to deal with Daniel ever again, that I could side-step disappointing my parents with the failure of my marriage. By simply slipping into oblivion, I wouldn't ever have to face learning to make my own way in the world. I just wasn't up for the struggle with all its emotional turmoil. I was just plumb tired.

"If you do this now, you won't be giving life a chance to get better."

My mind heard these words distinctly, but I knew I hadn't formed that thought; it was divine. I looked up instead of down and noticed a triangle formed by three faint stars. As night fell, I watched in silence and wonder as the stars brightened and the bottom of the canyon faded away.

Then I heard a voice echoing over the vast expanse. I couldn't see her, but I could hear her song strengthening as she rendered beautiful old tunes from the forties. I could also hear someone trying to hush her.

"Shhh," I heard him say. He half laughed and added, "People can hear you."

She sang louder. I loved that she paid him no mind. Her songs filled me with joy. Her determination changed my mood from despair to one of hopeful resilience.

They must have been sitting just behind the bushes around the bend. I couldn't see them, but I could hear her clearly. To my delight, she started belting out my absolute favorite song of all time, *Today* by Randy Sparks.

This song, about living in the moment and cherishing every fleeting moment of happiness, has always been special to me. I've loved it since I was a teenager. It gave me hope and the fact that she sang in spite of her man's disapproval gave me the idea that someday I could be brave like her. On the last verse I sang along with her, letting my voice mingle with hers across the chasm and back again. On the last line, I heard the bushes crackle and saw her come through to my little hideaway. We hugged. She was taller than me and slender, but her arms imparted a surprising strength.

She invited me back to the campsite. I thanked her politely, but I wanted to be on my way, hoping to reach California before depleting my quickly dwindling funds. We hugged again.

She'll never know how her songs gave me hope and saved my life. I will remember her and her voice for as long as I live. In my reveries, she's still voicing music that is both loud and proud.

TIME
Kathy Chencharik

"Father, I've lost track of Time," Millie Second said.

"If I've told you once, I've told you a thousand times, Time needs to be watched every minute of every day."

"But I only turned my back for a second."

"I don't care if it takes a week or even a year, you best get out there and find him."

"Yes, Father."

"And don't come back until you do."

Millie Second started up her time machine and went out in search of Time. She drove through the neighborhood, stopping to ask if anyone had seen her dog.

"Long time no see," good-Time Charlie said with a smile when Millie stopped to ask him. "How have you been?"

"Truth be told, I've been better," Millie said. "Right now I'm having a rough time. My father won't let me go home until I find Time. Have you seen him?"

Charlie put a hand to his chin in thought. "As a matter of fact, I believe I did see him enter those woods across the way." Charlie pointed. "He was following that trail."

"Thanks for taking the time to help me," Millie said as she parked her time machine and headed for the woods on foot.

Up ahead, she spotted an old-timer, a man with long white hair. "Excuse me sir, but have you seen a dog? It's getting late and I'm running out of time. Soon it will be dark and I need to find him before I can go home."

The old-timer pointed toward some bushes. "Well, it's about time," Millie said with a laugh as she watched the bushes shake and noticed her dog's tail moving them about.

"Thank you, sir. It looks like he's having a whale of a time, doesn't it?" As much as Millie hated to take away his fun, she called his name. Time ran out. "Come on boy," she said as she patted his head, "it's time to go home."

As Millie was about to enter the house, her father appeared in the doorway. "Well?"

Millie smiled and patted her leg. Her dog rushed over and sat beside her. "Time is on my side," she said as she brought her dog into the house. "And I won't let Time slip away again."

TROUBLE IN A FLASH
Diane Kane

I strolled down the sidewalk in my rural hometown, with a foreboding feeling. My eyes scanned familiar sights. With last week's frost, the majestic maples that lined the common had already passed from bright orange to the color of the crusty edges of my grandma's apple crisp. I paused on the bridge that traverses the river and inhaled the pungent oxygen that the water exhaled. There was no apparent reason for my discomfort in this serene setting.

Matters changed when I turned the corner, and the sound of a woman's scream broke the silence. "You!" a man shouted as he ran toward me. "You fit the description of the person we've been looking for."

I never imagined that I would be invited to be an extra in the filming of Castle Rock.

RESERVOIR OF MEMORY
Charlotte I. Taylor

back then, no one saw beavers
only gnawed evidence at the base of trees
the eagle was extinct and loons weren't real

lake fairies were common under the still surface
tiny things that rode water horses with manes like milfoil
darting between curled meadows and forests of green
a second look only tangled weeds and sunfish
the lake monster lifted his head from shadowy depths
submerged again on silent scales

Mom took me to the end of the bay
where the stream fed the lake
and invisible hands stacked fresh cut logs
the dam came into being as if with magic

the stream slowed and spread
giant puddles
took the trees
leaves fell and didn't return with spring
sunbeams flooded deepening trails of water
until shadow loving ferns and ginger gave way to grasses
branches broke, fell
naked grey trunks reached for the heavens

on the lake we canoed
to capture cattails and water lilies
and debate how to extract edible spatterdock roots
the fairies liked the swampy ends of the lake

The pond aged and changed
I counted bats and stars dancing
explored new places on the lake
knowing that my pond would always be there

I found places where rock erupted from earth
pondered God and Gods and an angry Goddess
who would tear open the earth and shoot cliffs upward
        I wondered at
shame and guilt and fear
that made her hide those scars with
a beauty of trees and ferns
as if it were a gift instead of a Fury

decades changed us
the pond grew herons settled
ducks and geese
turtles

water fairies more solitary until rarely seen
the lake monster nothing more than a story

canoes became kayaks and motor boats multiplied
a float plane touched the surface of the lake and rose again
fireworks to gunshots gunshots to cannons cannons to

Explosion
        the beaver dam blew
        The pond bled slowly back into lake

There are Beaver in the lake
I see them now
Otters play
I've even watched an Eagle
and heard the call of a Loon

There is a new magic
more footprints
and noise
and
        my mother sleeps beneath the Myrtle
        beside the water and the Elder

OUR CONTRIBUTORS

THE FOUNDER OF QUABBIN QUILLS

Steven Michaels is the author of *Sweet Life of Mystery*, a parody of the whodunit genre. He has been featured on *The Satirist* website for his scintillating take on current affairs, and has written over twenty plays for students as school director for the Drama Club. Steve founded the Quabbin Quills to ensure that the art of writing would long endure in and around this area for many years to come. He and other writers featured in this book came together to showcase the talent of local authors in their first anthology of *Time's Reservoir*.

ABOUT OUR PUBLISHER

Garrett Zecker is the publisher and co-founder of Quabbin Quills. He holds an MA in English from Fitchburg State University and an MFA in Fiction from Southern New Hampshire University. He founded Perpetual Imagination in 2004, specializing in independent releases and live events. Garrett is a writer, actor, and teacher of writing and literature. Links to much of his work, including full Shakespeare in the Park performances, can be found at the movie blog he co-writes with his wife, http://www.beforewediefilms.com.

ABOUT OUR ILLUSTRATOR

North Quabbin resident **Emily Boughton** has been rooted in the worlds of art and literature throughout her life. Her most prominent project to date is the interactive book and exhibit *Figure Me Out*, where she merges her love of design, photography, and writing into a self-reflective experience. When she is not working with youth at her local library, Emily enjoys filling her latest sketchbook with new ideas and doodles.

ABOUT OUR STORY EDITOR

Miryam Ehrlich Williamson is a former newspaper reporter and magazine writer. She is the author of a book on artificial intelligence, five books on health and longevity, and several published poems and short stories. Her work has won awards from the Associated Press and the American Medical Writers Association.

ABOUT OUR POETRY EDITORS

After a career in high-tech, **bg Thurston** now lives on a farm in Warwick, Massachusetts. Her first book, *Saving the Lamb*, by Finishing Line Press was a Massachusetts Book Awards highly recommended reading choice. Her second book, *Nightwalking*, was released in 2011 by Haleys. Currently, she is writing the history of the 1780's farmhouse she lives in. She teaches poetry workshops year-round, except in March when she is busy with lambing season.

Charlotte Taylor has published both short stories and poetry. She loves the process of creating with words and enjoys sharing the craft of writing with others. Charlotte is the writing persona for OPENArt+Yoga and is an active blogger for her work in Ayurveda, yoga, and writing. Musingclio.wordpress.com She is actively seeking a life of peace, study, and fun. Charlotte can often be found surrounded by cats with a mug of tea and reading books. Other times, you'll find her climbing mountains or crawling under barbed wire.

elaine reardon is a poet, herbalist, educator, and member of the Society of Children's Book Writers & Illustrators. Her chapbook, *The Heart is a Nursery For Hope*, published September 2016, recently won first honors from Flutter Press. Most recently elaine's poetry has been published in Three Drops from a Cauldron Journals and anthology, MA Poet of the Moment, **http://www.naturewriting.com**, and Poppy Road Review. She's also listed at **http://www.masspoetry.org/poemofthemoment5/#rpoms** Website: **elainereardon.wordpress.com**

Sharon A. Harmon is a freelance writer and poet. She has been published in *Birds & Blooms*, *Chicken Soup for the Soul* and *The Uniquely Quabbin Magazine*, as well as numerous other publications. Her second chapbook of poetry, *Wishbone in a Lightning Jar* was recently published and she attends many poetry venues. She lives with her husband deep in the woods of Royalston, and she is thrilled to see her story *Getting It Right* published in The Quabbin Quills Anthology.

ABOUT OUR AUTHORS

Bonnie Arnot grew up in New Jersey. After college, she moved to western Massachusetts, which had felt like home to her since the age of six when she first visited her grandparents in Athol. Bonnie married and raised two sons. She is currently seeking an agent to represent her work as a novelist.

Kathy Chencharik has had articles, poetry, and fiction published in numerous newspapers and magazines. She won the 2011 Derringer Award for Best Flash Story for "The Book Signing," published in *Thin Ice: Crime Stories by New England Writers*.

Phyllis Cochran has been writing and publishing stories for over twenty years. She has run writers' workshops and taught classes on "Writing for Publication." Her memoir, *Shades of Light*, was published in 2006. Phyllis enjoys spending time with family and friends, caring for her great-grandchildren and walking family member's dogs.

Joanne McIntosh has lived in Chelmsford most of her life and moved to Athol four years ago. She attended Mt. Wachusett Community College and Fitchburg State University, and after graduation, taught the sixth grade in Ayer. Joanne is now a Life Coach for Kids and an author of children's books. She is an active member of the Montachusett Suicide Prevention Task Force, the Heywood Healthcare Charitable Foundation, Quabbin Writers, the Berkshire Women Writers Group in Stockbridge, and the Society of Children's Book Writers and Illustrators. Joanne has a grown daughter and a teenage granddaughter who live in Grafton. Simba, a 35 pound Maine Coon cat, lives with her, and they both love exploring new exciting places in the North Quabbin.

Joshua DeVault is a poet from western Massachusetts. Inspired by nature and everyday life, Joshua tries to tie these themes in his writing. If away from the pen, you can find him hiking wooded trails or fishing by a lake.

Linda Donaldson is a graduate of the University of Massachusetts and former editor of the RVDA News. She is an educator and has been recognized by Literacy Volunteers of America for her devotion to Tutor Training. Linda is a proud homeowner in Athol where she works as an Executive Secretary. She is an avid reader who enjoys gardening, family gatherings, and mystery rides.

Clare Green, a retired educator, and perpetual amateur naturalist, invites folks to visit her woodland labyrinth and fairy cottage in Warwick, Mass. Her self-published books are available for purchase at Petersham Art Center.

Diane Kane writes short stories and poetry. Her self-published children's book, *Brayden the Brave* is featured at Boston Children's Hospital to help families dealing with medical issues. She belongs to two writers groups and enjoys sharing the love of writing with others. Diane has been published in Goose River Anthology and is one of the co-producers, as well as the submission coordinator of *Time's Reservoir*, a Quabbin Quills Anthology.

Dennis F. King started writing short stories three years ago. He enjoys recalling memories of his life experiences. A top computer tech for the Raytheon Co., now retired, has three sons and three grandchildren he adores. It is his opinion that writing is as easy as talking.

Clare Kirkwood, a graduate of the Culinary Institute of America, is a freelance food and beverage writer for the Uniquely Quabbin Magazine. Clare recently published a feature article in Porsche 356 Registry Magazine and currently serves on the board of directors for the Quabbin Quills Anthology.

Mary Owen's life has been a journey of light. She has worked as a counselor in women's shelters and homeless shelters in the Detroit area. In 2008 she answered the call to become an ordained Elder in the United Methodist Church and now pastors a church congregation in Athol, Massachusetts. In her quest for the truth of her beginnings, she is currently researching her heritage. She has two adult children and five grandchildren. Mary's life mission is to sow seeds of God's hope and love, to bring light into a dark world.

Sally Sennott is a graduate of Duke University. She was a long time resident of Athol and recently moved to southern New Hampshire. She is a retired newspaper correspondent and editor of a local museum newsletter. Sally has written two plays as well as a children's story that were produced into videos and featured on the Athol cable access channel (AOTV).

James Thibeault is the author of the novel *Deacon's Folly*, as well as the author of several short stories that have appeared in many literary journals and anthologies. He has been an English teacher for just under a decade and has been a resident of Massachusetts for all of his life.